The Ultimate THREAD GUIDE

Everything You Need to Know to Choose the Perfect Thread for Every Project

Becky Goldsmith

C&T PUBLISHING

Text copyright © 2019 by Becky Goldsmith

Photography and artwork copyright © 2019 by C&T Publishing, Inc.

Publisher: Amy Barrett-Daffin

Creative Director: Gailen Runge

Acquisitions Editor: Roxane Cerda

Managing/Developmental Editor: Liz Aneloski

Technical Editor: Helen Frost

Cover/Book Designer: April Mostek

Production Coordinator: Tim Manibusan

Production Editor: Jennifer Warren

Illustrator: Becky Goldsmith

Photo Assistants: Rachel Holmes and Gregory Ligman

Photography by Nissa Brehmer, Kelly Burgoyne, Christina Carty-Francis, Estefany Gonzalez, Rachel Holmes, Diane Pedersen, and Mai Yong Vang of C&T Publishing, Inc., unless otherwise noted below

Mettler-provided photography: Bottom of pages 8, 34, and 38

Shutterstock photography: Pages 1 and 42–63 (by Bankrx), 2 and 3 (by EKramar), 5 (by Kostikova Natalia), 10 (by savva_25), 13 (by Thaloengsak), 15 (by AVN Photo Lab), 22 and 23 (by Okskaz), 32 (by Africa Studio), 33 (by Alena TS), and 36 and 37 (by pan demin); top of pages 21 (by EKramar) and 8, 20, 24, 30, 34, and 40 (by 5 second Studio); center of page 12 (by fotohunter); right side of page 14 (by AVN Photo Lab); and bottom of pages 11 (by Cole Eaton Photography), 12 (by Baronb), 16 (by Calin Tatu), and 20 (by Stastny_Pavel)

Published by C&T Publishing, Inc., P.O. Box 1456, Lafayette, CA 94549

10 9 8 7 6 5 4 3 2

Introduction

When I learned to sew, it was easy to choose thread because there were very few choices. Times have changed. Now you get to (*have to*) choose between cotton, cotton/poly, nylon, polyester, rayon, silk, and wool threads. And the choices don't end there—you also have to choose the correct thread weight. It's enough to make you wilt in front of the thread display!

It is high time to make it simpler to find the right thread, and this guide will help you do just that.

Thread Types and Fibers

Should you only use cotton thread with cotton fabric? Is polyester bad? If you bring up these questions with sewing friends, be ready for a lively discussion!

After much research, I am happy to report that cotton, polyester, silk, wool, and other synthetic threads are all good when used properly. Once you understand the differences between the fibers, choosing the best thread for the job is a lot easier.

THREAD TYPES

Spun Thread

Cotton thread is made from short cotton fibers that are twisted together into strands, plies, and thread.

Spun polyester thread is manufactured in a similar way: Long polyester fibers are cut into shorter fibers that are twisted into single strands, which can be used together or with continuous filaments.

Spun threads produce lint in varying amounts.

Continuous-Filament Thread

Filaments are long, thin, unbroken strands of silk or a synthetic material that are twisted together to make thread. This type of thread is strong, smooth, and lint free.

Core-Spun Thread

Core-spun threads combine the strength of polyester with the sewability of cotton. Polyester filament centers are wrapped with spun-cotton or polyester fibers into strands that are then twisted together to form a plied thread. The filament core adds strength; the shorter fibers mimic 100% cotton thread. Core-spun threads can produce lint.

Monofilament Thread

This thread is a single strand of polyester fiber—like fishing line but much finer. Monofilaments usually come in clear and smoke for use on light and dark fabrics, respectively.

THREAD FIBERS

Natural Fibers

Natural fibers come from plants and animals. The three most common natural fibers used in home sewing are cotton, silk, and wool.

COTTON

Cotton is strong, has a light sheen, and tolerates high heat. It has a natural tooth that helps the thread to grab the fabric and stay in the seam. Cotton thread does produce lint in varying degrees.

Cotton fibers are judged by staple length, color, and character (how strong and resilient the fibers are). The better a cotton scores in all these areas, the higher the grade and the more expensive it is.

Egyptian cotton grown in Egypt is widely regarded as the best long-staple cotton due to the climate and soil conditions. Egyptian-grown cotton has longer staples (fibers) and is thinner and stronger than cotton grown in other places.

Egyptian cotton grown in other parts of the world complies with the Egyptian staple-length standard (1.25″–1.9″), but it is not necessarily of the same quality, color, or character.

Pima and Supima cotton are extra-long–staple cottons that originated in Egypt. In the early 1900s, a top-quality variety, known as *Pima*, was grown in Arizona and was named to honor the Pima Indians who tended the fields. Pima cotton is now grown in many countries; Supima is only grown in the United States.

It is difficult to look at a spool of thread and see whether the cotton itself is low or high quality. Price is a pretty good indicator of thread quality, as is the reputation of the manufacturer.

SILK

The best-known silk comes from the cocoons of mulberry silkworm larvae. Silk is unwound from the cocoon in one long continuous fiber.

Filament silk thread, considered to be the best, is made from multiple long strands of silk twisted together. Filament silk is strong, is lint free, and has a natural sheen. Be aware that silk, when subjected to UV exposure from sunlight, can discolor and become brittle.

WOOL

Wool fibers are graded by fineness, length, color, and appearance, fineness being the most important quality. Once sheared from the sheep, the fibers are cleaned, scoured, carded, and spun to make thread or yarn of various thicknesses. Wool thread is fuzzy.

Wool is often blended with acrylic fibers in thread for affordability and to add strength.

Regenerated Fibers

RAYON

Rayon was designed to mimic silk but come at a lower cost. It has a sateen sheen and is lint free.

Rayon is the most commonly used regenerated thread. It is extracted from naturally occurring cellulose that has been derived from wood pulp. Rayon is not a completely natural fiber because the cellulose requires extensive processing to become thread.

Cellulose is combined with a variety of chemicals into a liquid, which is extruded through spinnerettes that shape the fiber, turning it into long, thin strands. These strands are spun, twisted, and processed into thread.

Tip Rayon is sometimes referred to as *viscose*.

SILCO

Silco, by WonderFil (page 60), is a regenerated fiber derived from cotton rather than wood pulp. It has a sateen sheen and is lint free.

Synthetic Fibers

Synthetic fibers are petroleum based and engineered to provide specific attributes, such as strength and luster. Various chemicals are put into a liquid state and extruded through spinnerettes to create strands, which are then spun, twisted, and processed into thread. Fiber shape is carefully controlled to produce a desired property. For example, trilobal polyester has three "lobes" to catch and reflect more light to make a very shiny thread.

HOW DO SYNTHETIC THREADS LAST OVER TIME?

Natural fibers have been used in textiles for centuries, and we know how they age. Synthetic fibers became available for common use by home sewers sometime around 1940. Synthetic threads are derived from petroleum products. I can find no *specific* research on the lifespan of synthetic sewing thread.

An article published August 28, 2018, in the *NY Times*, "These Cultural Treasures Are Made of Plastic. Now They're Falling Apart." by XiaoZhi Lim, reported that art and artifacts made from synthetic materials housed in museum collections are seriously degrading. The damage caused is unpredictable and variable.

Every thread, natural or synthetic, has positive and negative characteristics. Fiber longevity is one more factor to consider when you choose thread.

HEAT TOLERANCE

Some synthetic threads may not tolerate high heat produced by your iron or clothes dryer. How hot is too hot? It's hard to know for a variety of reasons:

1. Iron temperatures vary.

2. Pressing seams open or in one direction has an impact on how hot the thread gets.

3. Ironing with steam increases the heat.

4. Dryer temperatures vary.

Watch for melting or brittle thread when ironing at high-heat settings and when using a new iron. When in doubt, iron at a lower temperature.

Tip Be a scientist and test your own thread! Place several strands of thread on cotton fabric and iron it on high heat. Let it cool and iron it again. Did it melt or change color? Is it brittle? Does it break easier if you tug it? Answering these questions can help you to make informed choices.

POLYESTER

Polyester is strong, smooth, and durable. It often has a sheen and can be lint free. Polyester  doesn't wrinkle or crease like cotton, which makes it a little slippery in the seam.

Contrary to what you may have heard, the polyester threads made today will not rip or tear your cotton fabric as long as you properly match the thread strength with the fabric.

Tip Seams sewn on a sewing machine with synthetic threads on top and in the bobbin can come "undone" when cut. To prevent this, switch the top thread to cotton and leave the polyester thread on the bobbin. The cotton grabs the fabric while the polyester leaves less lint in the bobbin area.

NYLON

Nylon is smooth, strong, and somewhat elastic. It melts at a lower temperature than polyester but may not melt with the heat generated by your home iron. Nylon, when subjected to UV exposure from the sun, can become discolored and brittle.

Nylon is sometimes blended with other fibers to add strength. Some invisible threads are made from 100% nylon.

Tip Nylon is also called *polyamide.*

ACRYLIC

Acrylic is a strong, synthetic fiber that is often blended with wool to add strength.

METALLIC AND MYLAR

Metallic thread is composed of a variety of materials that can be natural and/or synthetic to give it a high metallic shine.

Mylar thread is flat and very reflective. It is made by bonding layers of Mylar (sometimes with other synthetic fibers). Metallic and Mylar threads can be sensitive to high heat.

Adjust the tension and sewing speed when using metallic and Mylar thread on the sewing machine. Make sure to use an appropriate needle (see the Needle Size column in the tables, pages 43, 45, 47–49, 51, 53–55, 57, 59, 61, and 63, for your particular thread).

Thread Weight

WEIGHT CLASSIFICATION SYSTEMS

The three most common systems for determining thread weight are Weight (also called the *Gunze Count Standard*), Number English (or count/ply), and Tex. *There are other systems, but honestly, the more you know, the more confusing it is.* When *wt.* is printed on a spool, it can refer to any of these systems.

No system is used universally, which is why weight numbers are confusing. The same thread could have a weight number calculated from each system— each number would be different, and all would be correct.

Fixed-Weight Systems

When weight is fixed, the higher the weight number, the finer the thread.

WT. OR WEIGHT

Wt. = Number of kilometers per kilogram

In this system, the weight per kilogram is fixed. If 30 kilometers of thread equals 1 kilogram, it is a 30wt. thread.

NUMBER ENGLISH OR COUNT/PLY

Ne. or Count/Ply = Number of hanks of thread that weigh 1 pound

1 hank = 840 yards

In this system, the weight per pound is fixed. The resulting number is the thread "count." When used properly, count and ply are listed together with a slash between them, like this: 50/3. Spools are sometimes marked "Ne."

Fixed-Length System

When length is fixed, the higher the number, the thicker the thread.

TEX

Tex number = Weight in grams of 1,000 meters of thread

In this system, the length of the thread is fixed. If 1,000 meters weighs 35 grams, the thread is a Tex 35.

Tip **IMPORTANT!** The weight numbers printed on spools have the most meaning within each individual company's collection of threads. When comparing threads from different companies, use weight numbers as a general guide only.

60 wt.

50 wt.

35 wt.

THREAD THICKNESS

When you buy thread, do you care how much it weighs? No. You want to know how thick and/or strong it is. Weight numbers are a *general* indicator of thickness. Use your eyes and fingers to carefully evaluate the thickness of threads.

Some thread manufacturers have begun to classify threads as fine, medium, and heavy. These categories are broad and nonspecific but do have a common-sense appeal.

Choosing the Right Thread

When choosing thread, always think about how you want to use it. How strong does it need to be? Do you want it to blend in or stand out? Use your eyes and fingers to compare your choices, and choose the weight that best fits your needs—regardless of the numbers on the spool.

COMPARING THREAD—HEAD TO HEAD

Looking at thread on the spool doesn't reveal enough. It's better to hold single strands in your hand to compare them. What are you looking for?

Thickness: Thick thread is more visible than fine thread.

Smoothness: An obvious twist adds visible texture; less twist looks smoother.

Fuzziness: A slight fuzz, as opposed to a smooth and shiny finish, helps thread blend into the fabric. However, fuzzy thread means more lint in the bobbin area.

When you compare threads of the same weight from different companies, you will find that they vary. The differences may be subtle, but they do make a difference depending on how you plan to use the thread.

When in doubt, sew with a new thread before you use it in a project.

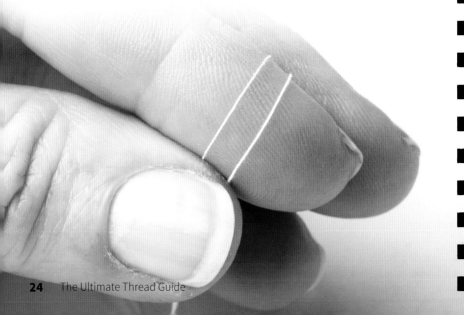

Detail of appliqué block by Becky Goldsmith

FINE THREAD

Fine thread is used for a variety of sewing tasks that include piecing, machine quilting, invisible hand appliqué, and English paper piecing. Fine threads are often 2-ply, but not all 2-ply threads are fine. If the plies are thick, the thread will also be thicker.

Fine thread can also be strong. The fiber the thread is made from helps to determine the strength of the thread.

ALL-PURPOSE THREAD

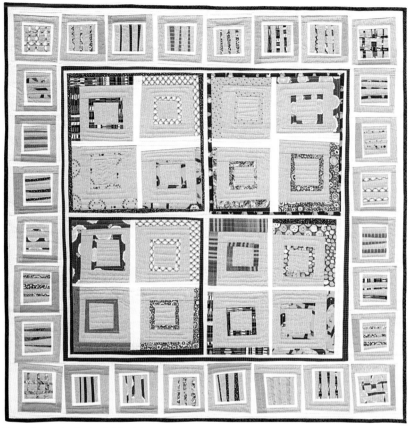

Brown Improv by Becky Goldsmith

All-purpose threads are generally medium-weight. They are strong and sometimes thick. You can use these threads for many sewing tasks, including machine piecing, garment and project sewing, and machine quilting.

When choosing thread for garments, bags, and other projects, take strength and durability into account. Polyester thread is used for commercially-made garments and bags and should be considered for similar projects that you make at home.

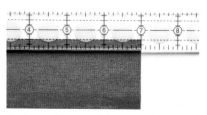

When precision is important, use a scant seam allowance with thicker thread. When you sew with a new thread, it's a good idea to double-check your seam allowance.

The thread is part of the seam allowance.

Starry Night by Amy Barrett-Daffin

Embroidery threads are meant to be seen!

EMBROIDERY THREAD

Embroidery thread can be made from cotton, polyester, rayon, wool, or silk and is available in a variety of weights. These threads can be used by hand or machine for embroidery, thread painting, machine quilting, and other kinds of embellishing stitches.

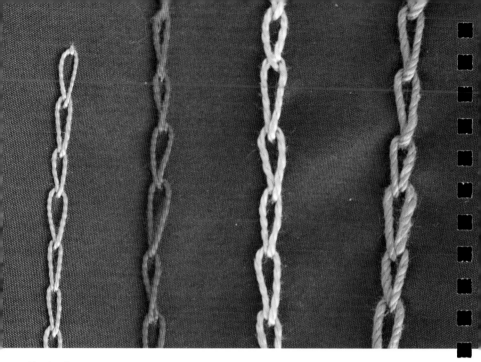

Perle Cotton

Perle cotton is a 2-ply thread that comes in five weights: 16, 12, 8, 5, and 3, with 16 being the thinnest and 3 being the thickest. It cannot be separated into thinner strands.

Perle cotton can be wound into balls and onto spools and can be used by hand or machine, depending on its thickness.

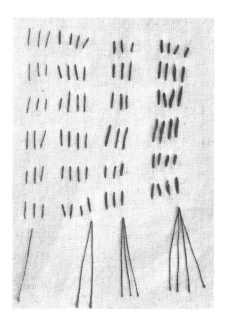

Embroidery Floss

Embroidery floss does not have a weight classification. Floss is comprised of three or six lightly twisted strands that can be easily separated. The soft twist gives the thread a very smooth appearance but also makes it more delicate.

MACHINE QUILTING THREAD

Detail of *Tile Tango* by Becky Goldsmith

A wide variety of threads are used in machine quilting. Consider the effect you want to achieve as you choose the thread.

• Fine threads have a low profile.

• Thick threads sit up higher on the fabric and call attention to themselves.

• Shiny threads reflect light and are more attention-grabbing.

• Low-luster threads blend into the fabric.

Be sure to choose a needle that is the correct size for the thread (see the Needle Size column in the tables, pages 43, 45, 47–49, 51, 53–55, 57, 59, 61, and 63, for your particular thread). If a thread is too thick for the top of your machine, you can sometimes sew with it on the bobbin.

Choosing the Correct Sewing Machine Needle

NEEDLE SIZES

Sewing machine needles have two numbers separated by a slash. The higher number is European; the smaller number is American. Longarm needles have three numbers: Longarm, American, and European.

For sewing machine needles, the bigger the number(s), the bigger the needle.

The reverse is true for hand-sewing needles, where larger numbers equal smaller needles.

Thread must sit fully in the groove of the needle without side-to-side movement. The eye of the needle must be large enough for the thread to pass through with as little friction as possible. Some thread manufacturers offer needle size and type suggestions; others do not.

SEWING MACHINE NEEDLES

European	American
60	8
70	10
75	11
80	12
90	14
100	16
110	18
120	20
130	22

LONGARM NEEDLES

Longarm	American	European
—	11	75
—	12	80
—	13	85
3.0	14	90
3.5	16	100
4.0	18	110
4.5	19–20	120
5.0	21–22	130

Tip When your sewing machine drops or skips stitches, it is often caused by needle damage or a mismatch between the size of the thread and the needle. Changing your needle may fix the problem.

MACHINE NEEDLE TYPES

Embroidery needles have an enlarged, polished eye and are designed for rayon and polyester threads.

Longarm needles are stronger to stand up to faster sewing speeds.

Metallic needles have an enlarged, polished eye to prevent shredding.

Microtex/sharps needles are slender and sharp for sewing straight stitches on most fabrics.

Quilting needles have a strong, tapered shaft to sew through multiple layers without breaking.

Topstitch needles have a very sharp point and an enlarged eye and groove for thicker threads.

Universal needles are less sharp and are tapered to glide through the fabric without pulling threads in the weave of the fabric.

Jeans/denim needles are heavy duty and designed to use with denim. You might also use them in machine quilting and other situations where a very strong needle is required.

Ballpoint needles have a rounded tip and are designed to use on jersey, stretch, and synthetic fabrics.

Leather needles have a sharp cutting point designed to pierce leather, artificial leather, and other thick nonwovens.

HAND NEEDLE TYPES

Sharps are short- to medium-length needles with sharp points that are used for a wide range of hand-sewing tasks.

Betweens are short, sharp needles used in hand quilting and other precise sewing situations.

Embroidery/crewel needles have sharp points and long eyes that are wider than the shaft of the needle. *Embroidery* refers to fancy stitches made with floss or thread. *Crewel* refers to the same stitches sewn with wool thread. The needle is the same in both cases.

Straw/milliners needles are long needles with round eyes that were traditionally used in hat making but are preferred by some who like a longer needle for hand sewing.

Tapestry needles have a large eye and a blunt, round point. They are used in needlepoint, petit point, counted cross-stitch, and plastic canvas work.

How Thread Is Made

Cotton fibers are cleaned, fluffed, combed, and spun together into thin strands that are then twisted together into plies. Plies are twisted together to make thread, which is then treated, dyed, and wound onto spools for sale.

Polyester fibers are processed differently from cotton, but they, too, can be spun and twisted together.

SPIN, TWIST, AND PLY

Short fibers (cotton and/or polyester) are spun together to make a continuous strand that is twisted to hold the fibers together. Strands are then twisted together to make a ply. Plies are then twisted together to form the final thread.

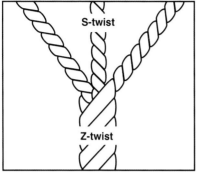

Strands are twisted in the S direction. Plies are twisted together in Z direction to balance out the S twist. The final twist for threads intended to be used on a sewing machine is always in the Z direction because of the way thread feeds off the spool and into the machine.

S and Z twists balance each other out.

Twists hold the fibers and strands together. If the twist is too low, thread can fray and break. If the twist is too high, thread can be unruly. Each manufacturer decides how thick to make the plies and how tightly to twist their thread.

2-ply Versus 3-ply

When the thread weight printed on the spool is followed by a slash, the second number tells you how many plies that thread has. The ply number may or may not be printed on the spool. In general, more plies

equals thicker thread.

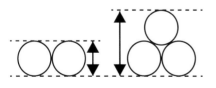

If you look at a cross section of 2- and 3-ply threads, you will see that 2-ply thread is flatter and 3-ply thread is shaped like a pyramid. The 2-ply thread has a flat profile and is not subject to as much wear and tear from abrasion. The 3-ply thread sits up taller on the fabric. It stands out visually and is subject to more abrasion.

GASSING

Gassing is the process in which thread is passed through a gas flame at high speed to burn off the longest fibers that stick out from the thread. The resulting thread is smoother and more lustrous.

MERCERIZATION

During *mercerization*, cotton fibers are immersed in a caustic solution that makes the fibers swell and accept dye more easily. Mercerization also makes the thread stronger and more lustrous.

Cotton thread is usually mercerized, whether it says so on the label or not.

DYEING

Historically, dyes came from animals or plants. In the mid-nineteenth century, people learned how to make artificial dyes in order to achieve a broader range of colors that were more colorfast. Different kinds of dyes are used for different fibers.

Commercially-dyed thread is made on a large scale in a sealed, pressurized vat. Liquid dye is pumped into the vat under pressure and raised to the dyeing temperature. The flow of dye inside the vat, the temperature, the timing, and the addition of chemicals are carefully controlled by computers for precise color matching.

Poly/cotton threads are made up of two different fibers, and each fiber requires a different kind of dye. This dyeing process is more complicated and takes longer. The two separate dye cycles are carried out one after the other in the same overall dyeing operation. Excess dye is removed using centrifuges, and the thread is dried using hot air or radio-frequency dryers.

Colorfastness

Colorfastness refers to how well a thread retains its color during normal use, and it has several components:

Washfastness: Does the thread lose color during laundering?

Crocking: Does color rub off when the thread is wet or dry?

Cold water migration: When wet thread sits on wet fabric, does dye migrate?

Lightfastness: Does thread fade when exposed to long periods of daylight?

Synthetic threads are generally more colorfast than cotton or rayon, but as conditions vary, so can colorfastness. When in doubt, test the thread before you use it.

FINISHES AND GLAZES

Heat is generated as thread passes through a sewing machine, especially through the eye of the needle. Many threads are coated with wax, oil, or silicone to smooth the thread, add luster, and help eliminate friction-related heat damage. The amount of finish applied to any thread is carefully controlled by the manufacturer.

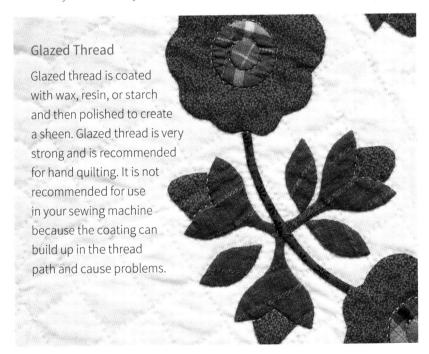

Glazed Thread

Glazed thread is coated with wax, resin, or starch and then polished to create a sheen. Glazed thread is very strong and is recommended for hand quilting. It is not recommended for use in your sewing machine because the coating can build up in the thread path and cause problems.

Thread Manufacturers

The information on the following pages was provided by the thread manufacturers and is a snapshot of the threads offered by these manufacturers at the time of printing. If you would like to know more, please look at each company's offerings online.

The thread-weight numbers in the charts correspond to the numbers on the spool or to information from the manufacturer. Ply numbers are not always listed on the spools. Whenever possible, I have included that information.

Tip Individual manufacturers often color-code their spools or labels to make it easier to differentiate between their thread offerings.

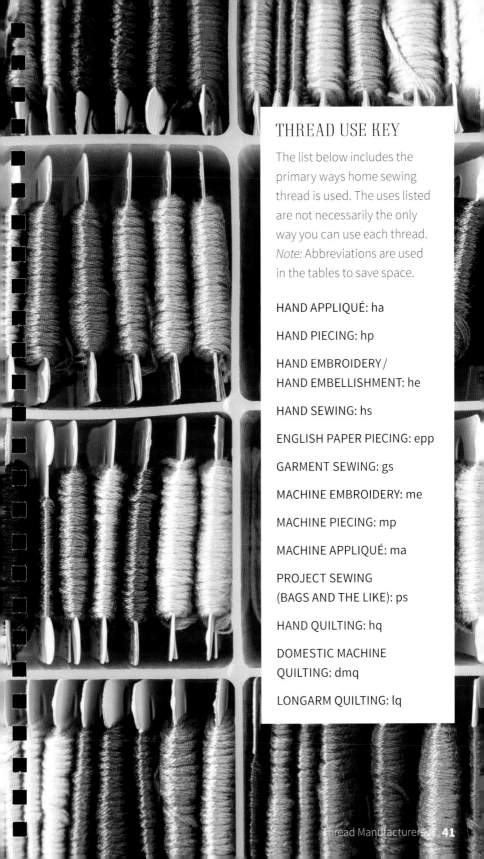

THREAD USE KEY

The list below includes the primary ways home sewing thread is used. The uses listed are not necessarily the only way you can use each thread. *Note:* Abbreviations are used in the tables to save space.

HAND APPLIQUÉ: ha

HAND PIECING: hp

HAND EMBROIDERY/
HAND EMBELLISHMENT: he

HAND SEWING: hs

ENGLISH PAPER PIECING: epp

GARMENT SEWING: gs

MACHINE EMBROIDERY: me

MACHINE PIECING: mp

MACHINE APPLIQUÉ: ma

PROJECT SEWING
(BAGS AND THE LIKE): ps

HAND QUILTING: hq

DOMESTIC MACHINE
QUILTING: dmq

LONGARM QUILTING: lq

Aurifil controls the manufacture of its thread from fiber to finished product. Their cotton thread is made with Egyptian-grown cotton from the Mako region, and all production occurs in the company's headquarters in Milan, Italy. Their cotton thread is strong, smooth, and available in up to 270 colors in a variety of weights.

Cotton 12wt is a heavy thread that can be used by hand and machine.

Cotton 28wt is a medium-weight thread that can be used by hand and machine.

Cotton 40wt is a 2-ply thread that is slightly thicker and perfect for those times when you need a stronger thread or greater definition.

Cotton 50wt is strong and fine and can be used by hand and machine.

Cotton 80wt is a delicate, fine thread. Use shorter lengths when hand sewing. Use thin, sharp needles and sew slowly on the machine.

Cotton Floss is a 6-ply thread wound on wooden spools to prevent tangles.

Cotton Forty3 is a 3-ply thread created especially for handling today's high-speed, high-tech longarm machines.

Monofilament is 100% nylon and comes in clear and smoke, rendering it nearly invisible on both light and dark projects.

Polyester Longarm is a variegated, high-sheen, strong polyester thread that won't break in your machine and doesn't produce lint.

Wool is a 50% wool, 50% acrylic blend. The wool provides a soft loft and the acrylic adds strength. Some spools may be labeled with "Lana," which means "wool" in Italian and Spanish.

Thread name	Fiber	Wt./ply	Use	Needle size
Cotton 80wt	Cotton	80/2	ha, epp, me, ma, dmq	70/10 or 80/12 microtex/sharps or embroidery
Cotton 50wt	Cotton	50/2	ha, hp, epp, gs, me, mp, ma, ps, dmq	80/12 microtex/sharps or universal; 4.0 longarm
Cotton 40wt	Cotton	40/2	hp, gs, me, ma, ps, dmq, lq	80/12 microtex/sharps or universal, 75/11 or 90/14 quilting; 3.5 or 4.0 longarm
Cotton Forty3	Cotton	40/3	gs, mp, ps, dmq, lq	90/14 or 100/16 topstitch; 4.0 or 4.5 longarm
Cotton 28wt	Cotton	28/2	hp, he, me, hq, dmq, lq	90/14 topstitch or quilting; 4.0 longarm
Cotton 12wt	Cotton	12/2	he, me, ma, dmq, lq	90/14 or 100/16 topstitch; 4.5 longarm
Cotton Floss	Cotton	6-strand floss	he	—
Polyester Longarm	Polyester	40/2	me, dmq, lq	80/12 microtex/sharps or universal; 3.5 or 4.0 longarm
Wool	Wool/acrylic	12/—	he, ma, dmq, lq	90/14 or 100/16 topstitch; 5.0 longarm
Monofilament	Nylon	—	ha, epp, ma, dmq, lq	90/14 or 100/16 universal, microtex/sharps, or embroidery; 4.0 longarm

COATS & CLARK

Coats & Clark has a global presence and produces thread for many different industries, including home sewing. Coats uses extra-long–staple Egyptian cotton.

Cotton All Purpose is designed for general sewing on natural fibers and is available in many colors.

Cotton Covered Bold Hand Quilting is a glazed 25% cotton-wrapped / 75% polyester-core thread in 10wt. that is designed for big-stitch handwork.

Cotton Covered Quilting & Piecing is a 40% cotton-wrapped / 60% polyester-core thread for the look of cotton with the strength of polyester.

Cotton Hand Quilting is glazed to prevent tangles and knots. It is not meant for use on a machine.

Cotton Machine Quilting comes in larger spools with more yardage.

Dual Duty Plus Hand Quilting is a glazed 32% cotton-wrapped / 68% polyester-core thread that is available in 20wt.

Dual Duty XP threads are polyester-covered polyester.

60wt. is lightweight for hand and fine machine sewing.

35wt. is intended for all-purpose sewing.

15wt. is heavy for extra strength.

Metallic Embroidery thread is 44% nylon, 34% metallic polyester, and 22% cotton.

Quilt+ Piecing & Quilting is made from extra-long–staple Egyptian cotton that has been double-mercerized for extra smoothness. It is designed for piecing and machine quilting.

Quilt+ Quilting & Embroidery and **Trilobal Embroidery** threads are trilobal, lint-free filament polyester designed for machine embroidery and machine quilting.

Transparent Polyester is a monofilament polyester designed for machine sewing.

Thread name	Fiber	Wt./ply	Use	Needle size
Cotton All Purpose	Cotton	30/3	hp, gs, mp, ps, dmq, lq	75/11, 90/14, 100/16, 110/18
Cotton Machine Quilting	Cotton	30/3	dmq, lq	75/11, 90/14
Quilt+ Piecing & Quilting	Cotton	30/3	hp, mp, dmq, lq	75/11, 90/14
Cotton Hand Quilting (glazed)	Cotton	20/3	hq	Betweens or sharps 7, 8, 9, or 10
Cotton Covered Quilting & Piecing	Cotton-covered polyester	35/3	mp, dmq, lq	75/11, 90/14, 100/16, 110/18
Dual Duty Plus Hand Quilting (glazed)	Cotton-covered polyester	25/2	hq	Not for machine use
Cotton Covered Bold Hand Quilting (glazed)	Cotton-covered polyester	10/3	hq	Not for machine use
Dual Duty XP Paper Piecing and Dual Duty XP Fine	Polyester-covered polyester	60/2	ha, hp, gs, mp, epp	65/9
Quilt+ Quilting & Embroidery	Polyester	40/2	me, dmq, lq	75/11
Dual Duty XP All Purpose	Polyester-covered polyester	35/2	hp, gs, mp, ps, dmq, lq	75/11, 90/14, 100/16
Dual Duty XP Heavy	Polyester-covered polyester	15/3	ps, dmq, lq	100/16, 110/18
Trilobal Embroidery	Polyester	40/2	me, dmq, lq	75/11
Transparent Polyester	Polyester	70/1	ma, dmq, lq	65/9
Metallic Embroidery	Nylon / metallic polyester / cotton	40/2	me, dmq, lq	75/11

Founded in 1978, Fil-Tec makes thread for home sewing and industrial uses. They dye, wind, and lubricate their thread in the United States. Fil-Tec uses long-staple Egyptian cotton that is mercerized, strong, smooth, and low lint.

Fil-Tec has a unique patented magnetic-core bobbin design that is available on most of their pre-wound bobbins. Plastic-sided bobbins are also available.

Affinity is a 40wt. polyester with 1˝ variegations.

Allure is a fine, strong 100wt. multifilament thread made from Japanese silk.

Cairo-Quilt is a 50wt. multipurpose Egyptian-grown cotton thread.

Essence is an invisible nylon monofilament. Avoid direct contact with an iron and high heat when laundering.

Glide 60 is finer filament polyester thread. It has a lower sheen than Glide.

Glide is a strong 40wt. trilobal polyester thread with a brilliant sheen.

Glisten is a 40wt. metallic-wrapped rayon.

Harmony is a 40wt. variegated cotton thread with color changes every 1˝.

Luminary is a glow-in-the-dark 40wt. polyester. The glow fades with repeated washing.

Medley is a 50wt. multipurpose thread with a polyester core wrapped with cotton.

Perish thread dissolves in cold water. Use it for basting and in trapunto, appliqué, and heirloom sewing when you want the thread to disappear when washed. Store in a ziplock bag and do not handle with wet hands!

Premo-Soft is a strong 50wt. thread with a filament core wrapped with spun polyester.

Thread name	Fiber	Wt./ply or size	Use	Needle size
Affinity	Polyester	40/2	me, dmq, lq	75/11; 4.0 longarm
Allure	Silk	100/2	ha, epp, dmq, lq	70/10; 3.0 longarm
Cairo-Quilt	Cotton	50/3	hp, gs, mp, ps, dmq, lq	90/14; 3.5 longarm
Essence— mini spool	Nylon monofilament	.004 mm or Tex 8	dmq, lq	70/10
Essence— king spool	Nylon monofilament	.008 mm or Tex 35	dmq, lq	100/16; 3.0 longarm
Glide 60	Polyester	60/2	hp, gs, mp, ps, dmq, lq	65/9; 4.0 longarm
Glide	Polyester	40/2	me, dmq, lq	75/11; 4.0 longarm
Glisten	Rayon/metallic	40/—	me, dmq, lq	90/14; 4.0 longarm
Harmony	Cotton	40/3	me, dmq, lq	90/14; 4.0 longarm
Luminary	Polyester	40/—	me, dmq, lq	75/11; 4.0 longarm
Medley	Polyester/cotton	50/2	hp, gs, mp, ps, dmq, lq	80/12; 3.5 longarm
Perish	Water soluble	40/—	—	80/12; 3.5 longarm
Premo-Soft	Polyester	50/3	hp, gs, mp, ps, dmq, lq	90/14; 4.0 longarm

GÜTERMANN

Cotton 12 is a heavy thread and can be used by hand and machine.

Cotton 30 is a thick thread and can be used by hand and machine.

Extra Strong M 782 is designed for heavy sewing.

Natural Cotton Ne 40 is an all-purpose thread that is mercerized for strength and luster.

Quilting is a cotton thread glazed for smooth, tangle-free sewing.

◈Gütermann

Rayon 40 is a soft and glossy thread designed for machine use.

Sew-All Thread is an all-purpose thread.

Silk S 303 is a fine thread that can be used by hand or machine.

Top Stitch is a soft, silky, and colorfast polyester thread designed for ornamental sewing.

Thread name	Fiber	Wt./ply	Use	Needle size
Natural Cotton Ne 40	Cotton	40/3	hp, gs, mp, ps, dmq, lq	70/10 or 80/12 universal
Cotton 30	Cotton	30/2	he, me, ps, dmq, lq	70/10 or 80/12 universal
Cotton 12	Cotton	18/2	he, me, dmq, lq	100/16 or 110/18 universal
Quilting (glazed)	Cotton	39/3	hq	Not for machine use
Sew-All Thread	Polyester	100/2	ha, gs, mp, ma, ps, dmq, lq	70/10, 80/12, or 90/14 universal
Extra Strong M 782	Polyester	40/2	gs, mp, ps, dmq, lq	70/10, 80/12, 90/14, or 100/16 universal
Top Stitch	Polyester	30/3	me, dmq, lq	100/16 or 120/18 universal
Rayon 40	Rayon	40/2	me, dmq, lq	70/10, 80/12, or 90/14 machine embroidery
Silk S 303	Silk	100/3	ha, mp, ma, dmq	70/10 or 80/12 universal

IRIS

Iris cotton threads are manufactured by Hilos Iris in Monterrey, Mexico.

Iris Dazzling Metallic has a nylon core wrapped with polyester metallic.

Perle cotton is a size 8, 2-ply thread made with 100% long-staple combed cotton.

So-Rite Corespun Polyester is strong and designed for all-purpose sewing.

UltraBrite Polyester is a strong American-made trilobal polyester that is dyed and wound in Mexico.

Ultra Cotton is made from long-staple Egyptian cotton that has been double-gassed and mercerized. Solid colors are suitable for high-speed sewing. Use variegated thread for slower sewing and hand quilting.

Thread name	Fiber	Wt./ply or size	Use	Needle size*
Iris Dazzling Metallic	Nylon core-poly wrapped	—	me, dmq, lq	90/14 embroidery
Perle cotton	Cotton	—/2, size 8	he, hq	—
So-Rite Corespun Polyester	Core-spun polyester	39/2	gs, me, mp, ps, dmq, lq	—
Ultra Cotton	Cotton	50/3	hp, gs, mp, hq, dmq, lq	—
UltraBrite Polyester	Polyester	40/—	me, dmq, lq	—

This company does not provide needle size recommendations for all thread types.

METTLER

Mettler is a global company, based in Germany, that controls the manufacture of its thread from fiber to finished product. Mettler uses Egyptian-grown long-staple cotton. Cotton thread is mercerized for strength and luster and is available in four weights for use in many applications.

Bobbinette (also known as **Bobbin Fil**) is a fine core-spun polyester thread that is available in white and black.

Cordonnet 30 is a strong polyester thread perfect for decorative sewing.

Metallic is 55% metallic polyester wrapped around a 45% nylon (polyamide) core.

Metrosene is an all-purpose core-spun polyester thread that is strong and smooth.

Poly Sheen is a trilobal polyester that will catch and reflect light. It can be laundered often.

Mettler ®

Thread.Color.Imagination.

Seracor is an all-purpose core-spun polyester thread with a strong core, around which smooth fibers are spun.

Seralene is a fine, smooth, continuous-filament, multipurpose polyester thread.

Silk-Finish Cotton 28 is strong and thick for beautiful decorative sewing by hand or machine.

Silk-Finish Cotton 40 is intended for all-purpose sewing.

Silk-Finish Cotton 50 is intended for all-purpose sewing.

Silk-Finish Cotton 60 is lightweight for hand and fine machine sewing.

Transfil is a nylon monofilament available in clear and smoke.

Thread name	Fiber	Wt./ply or size	Use	Needle size
Bobbinette (Bobbin Fil)	Polyester	60/2	ha, hp, mp, gs, ps	60/8, 70/10
Metallic	Polyester/nylon	40/—	me, dmq, lq	70/10, 80/12
Metrosene	Polyester	50/2	ha, gs, mp, ma, ps, dmq, lq	80/12, 90/14
Cordonnet 30	Polyester	30/3	me, ps, dmq, lq	110/18
Poly Sheen	Polyester	40/2	me, ps, dmq, lq	70/10, 80/12
Seracor	Polyester	50/2	ha, gs, mp, ma, ps, dmq, lq	70/10, 80/12
Seralene	Polyester	60/2	ha, gs, me, mp, ma, ps, dmq, lq	65/9, 70/10
Silk-Finish Cotton 60	Cotton	60/2	ha, hp, me, ma, dmq, lq	70/10, 80/12
Silk-Finish Cotton 50	Cotton	50/2	ha, gs, mp, ma, ps, dmq, lq	80/12, 90/14
Silk-Finish Cotton 40	Cotton	40/2	ha, gs, mp, ma, ps, dmq, lq	80/12, 90/14
Silk-Finish Cotton 28	Cotton	28/2	he, me, ps, hq, dmq, lq	110/18, 130/22
Transfil	Nylon monofilament	.00055 optical diameter	me, mp, ma, dmq, lq	80/12, 90/14

Presencia cotton threads are made from extra-long–staple cotton grown in the Giza region of Egypt. Color conversion charts for DMC and Anchor floss numbers are available online.

Cotton sewing/quilting threads are mercerized, colorfast, shrinkfast, and virtually lint free. Mouline Special Finca embroidery floss and Finca perle cotton threads are bleachfast, mercerized, colorfast, and shrinkfast.

The Spanish and French words *finca* and *mouliné* (found on many of the labels) are used together to mean "embroidery floss."

Finca perle cotton is available in 5 sizes (16, 12, 8, 5, and 3) and 122 solid and 33 variegated colors.

Metallic Floss is a 6-strand divisible thread with a polyester core that is wrapped with metal fiber. It is shred resistant. Strands can be separated and used alone or with other flosses.

Metallic Thread has a polyester core wrapped with metal fiber and is available in skeins, spools, and cones. Metallic Thread does not work well on any high-speed machines. Use only domestic machines at a low speed.

Mouline Special Finca embroidery floss comes in 6-strand skeins and 122 solid and 33 variegated colors.

Sewing Thread 40/3 is a heavier thread for machine and longarm quilting.

Sewing Thread 50/3 is a strong multipurpose thread.

Sewing Thread 60/3 is lightweight for fine stitching.

Thread name	Fiber	Wt./ply or size	Use	Needle size*
Sewing Thread 60/3	Cotton	60/3	ha, hp, mp, ma, dmq	—
Sewing Thread 50/3	Cotton	50/3	hp, gs, mp, ps, dmq	—
Sewing Thread 40/3	Cotton	40/3	he, me, dmq, lq	—
Mouline Special Finca embroidery floss	Cotton	—/6	he	—
Metallic Floss	Polyester/metallic	—/6	he	—
Metallic Thread	Polyester/metallic	—/1 and 2	he, dmq	—
Finca perle cotton	Cotton	—/2; sizes 16, 12, 8, 5, 3	he, hq	—

This company does not provide needle-size recommendations.

These threads come with Alex Anderson's seal of approval. No needle sizes are suggested.

Para-Cotton Poly is a fine 100% polyester that has been thermally treated to make the thread behave and look more like mercerized cotton.

Perfect Cotton Plus combines Egyptian cotton with polyester for added strength.

Thread name	Fiber	Wt./ply	Use	Needle size*
Para-Cotton Poly	Polyester	80/2	ha, hp, me, ma	—
Perfect Cotton Plus	Cotton-covered polyester	60/2	hp, mp, ma	—

* This company does not provide needle-size recommendations.

STAR (YLI THREADS)

Star Cotton (from YLI Threads) is an all-purpose thread made from extra-long–staple Egyptian cotton. It is dyed in North Carolina, Georgia, or Japan and then finished, wound, and packaged in South Carolina. It is

available in solid and variegated colors. No needle sizes are suggested.

Thread name	Fiber	Wt./ply	Use	Needle size*
Star Cotton	Cotton	50/3	hp, gs, me, mp, ma, dmq, lq	—

* This company does not provide needle-size recommendations.

SULKY

Sulky uses 100% Egyptian-grown long-staple cotton.

12 Wt. Cotton is a thick, decorative thread.

30 Wt. Cotton is designed to make a bold statement.

40 Wt. Rayon has a silklike luster, is strong, and has less stretch than polyester.

Cotton + Steel is an all-purpose thread made from Egyptian cotton.

Holoshimmer Metallic is a thin, flat polyester film made with a holographic layer.

Invisible Polyester is a soft, fine monofilament polyester thread.

Original Metallic thread features metallic fibers twisted around a polyester core.

Poly Deco and **PolyLite** are trilobal, continuous-filament, shiny polyester threads.

Sliver Metallic is a thin, flat polyester film with an aluminum layer to add reflectiveness.

Thread name	Fiber	Wt./ply or size	Use	Needle size
Cotton + Steel	Cotton	50/—	ha, hp, me, mp, ma, dmq	75/11, 80/12, or 90/14 quilting, microtex, or embroidery
Holoshimmer Metallic	Polyester and metallic	—	he, me, dmq	90/14 metallic or topstitch
Original Metallic	Polyester and metallic	—	he, me, dmq, lq	90/14 metallic or topstitch
PolyLite	Polyester	60/—	ha, me, mp, dmq, lq	75/11 embroidery
Poly Deco	Polyester	40/—	me, mp, dmq, lq	80/12 or 90/16 embroidery
Sliver Metallic	Polyester and metallic	—	he, me, dmq	90/14 metallic or topstitch
30 Wt. Cotton	Cotton	30/—	he, hq, dmq, lq	90/14 quilting or topstitch
12 Wt. Cotton	Cotton	12/—	he, hq, dmq, lq	100/16 denim or topstitch
Invisible Polyester	Polyester	.004 mm	ma, dmq, lq	75/11, 80/12, or 90/14 embroidery
40 Wt. Rayon	Rayon	40/—	he, me, dmq, lq	80/12, 90/14

Superior's cotton threads are made from Egyptian-grown extra-long–staple cotton fibers.

Bottom Line polyester thread is fine, strong, and lint free.

Fantastico, Living Colors, Magnifico, Nature Colors, Rainbows, and **Super Brights** are strong trilobal polyester threads with a high sheen. Fantastico is variegated with a 1″ color-change interval.

Glitter is a flat, metallized, shimmery polyester thread made from a thin layer of polyester film adhered to holographic Mylar.

Kimono Silk is a smooth, strong filament silk thread.

King Tut is made from Egyptian-grown extra-long–staple cotton and is designed for quilting and decorative stitching.

MasterPiece Egyptian-grown extra-long–staple cotton thread is designed for piecing, sewing, and quilting. It is finished in a 3-ply thread on the spool or cone and as a 2-ply thread on pre-wound bobbins (called **SuperBOBs**).

Metallics is made from a blend of raw materials in a unique process to make it vibrant, strong, and smooth.

MicroQuilter is an extrafine filament polyester thread.

MonoPoly is a reduced-sheen mono-filament polyester thread that is available in Clear and Smoke.

OMNI and **OMNI-V** are strong poly-wrapped poly core (core-spun) threads.

Quilter's Silk is a heavy, strong filament silk thread.

Sew Sassy is a 3-ply polyester thread with a matte finish designed for wool appliqué.

So Fine! is a strong, lint-free multifilament polyester thread with a medium sheen.

Tiara Silk is a fine, strong, lint-free filament silk thread with a high sheen.

Tire Silk is available as a 50wt. and a 30wt. thread. Both are smooth, strong filament threads.

Treasure cotton is a glazed cotton thread for hand quilting.

Twist is a trilobal polyester thread in which 2 separately-dyed polyester filaments have been combined to create a 40wt. 2-ply, dual-color thread.

Thread name	Fiber	Wt./ply	Use	Needle size
Glitter	—	40/—	me, dmq, lq	90/14
Kimono Silk	Silk	100/2	ha, ma, dmq, lq	60/8, 70/10
King Tut	Cotton	40/3	me, dmq, lq	90/14
Fantastico, Living Colors, Magnifico, Nature Colors, Rainbows, and Super Brights	Polyester	40/2	he, me, dmq, lq	90/14
MasterPiece on spools and cones	Cotton	50/3	hp, me, mp, ma, dmq, lq	80/12
MasterPiece on pre-wound bobbins (SuperBOBs)	Cotton	50/2	ha, hp, me, mp, ma, dmq	—
Metallics	—	40/—	he, me, dmq, lq	90/14
MicroQuilter	Polyester	100/2	ha, gs, me, mp, ma, dmq, lq	70/10
MonoPoly	Polyester	100/—	ma, dmq, lq	70/10
OMNI and OMNI-V	Core-spun polyester	40/2	hp, he, me, mp, dmq, lq	90/14
Quilter's Silk	Silk	16/3	he, me, dmq, lq	100/16
Sew Sassy	Polyester	12/3	he, me	100/16
So Fine! #60	Polyester	60/3	ha, all machine sewing	Pre-wounds only
So Fine! #50	Polyester	50/3	ha, gs, me, mp, ma, dmq, lq	80/12
So Fine! #40	Polyester	40/3	he, me, dmq, lq	90/14
So Fine! #30	Polyester	30/3	he, me, dmq, lq	100/16
Bottom Line	Polyester	60/2	ha, gs, me, mp, ma, dmq, lq	60/8, 70/10
Treasure (glazed)	Cotton	30/3	hq	Not for machine use
Twist	Polyester	40/2	he, me, dmq, lq	90/14
Tiara Silk	Silk	50/2	he, me, dmq, lq	80/12
Tire Silk #50	Silk	50/3	he, me, mp, dmq, lq	80/12
Tire Silk #30	Silk	30/3	he, me, dmq, lq	100/16

All Valdani threads are hand-dyed and guaranteed colorfast in all their colors.

3-Strand Cotton Floss, created by Valdani, is perfect for punch needle.

6-Strand Cotton Floss is excellent for cross-stitch, embroidery, crazy quilting, and fringe and tassel making.

6-Strand Silk Floss has the strength and high sheen of pure silk.

35wt. Cotton is designed for both machine and hand quilting; being heavier, it is highly decorative.

50wt. Cotton is a slightly heavier multipurpose sewing thread.

60wt. Cotton thread is equivalent to regular sewing thread.

Art Silk Rayon Floss, an indivisible rayon floss, is a high-luster decorative thread for hand embroidery and Brazilian embroidery.

Brilliance is a strong filament polyester thread with a high sheen.

CottonLook is a spun polyester thread that has the look and feel of cotton but the tolerance of polyester.

Machine Embroidery Rayon thread is designed for home and high-speed machine embroidery.

Merino Virgin Wool is 100% Australian wool and comes in sizes 15 and 8. Use it for wool appliqué and hand stitching.

Perle Cotton in sizes 12 (fine), 8 (medium), and 5 (heavy) is designed for all hand embroidery and wool appliqué.

Perle Silk (pearl silk) is a strong mulberry silk thread with a natural sheen that is hand-dyed and wound on spools for both hand and machine sewing.

Unique Twist is a blend of 1-ply poly and 1-ply cotton. The cotton is hand-dyed for a "fluffy" look.

Thread name	Fiber	Wt./ply or size	Use	Needle size*
35wt. Cotton	Cotton	35/—	he, me, hq, dmq, lq	90/14
50wt. Cotton	Cotton	50/—	hp, mp, gs, dmq, lq	—
60wt. Cotton	Cotton	60/—	ha, hp, gs, mp, dmq, lq	—
3-Strand Cotton Floss	Cotton	—/3	he, punch needle	—
6-Strand Cotton Floss	Cotton	—/6	he	—
6-Strand Silk Floss	Silk	—/6	he	110/18
Art Silk Rayon Floss	Rayon	—/10	he	—
Brilliance	Polyester	40/—	he, me, dmq, lq	—
CottonLook	Polyester	40/—	dmq, lq	—
Perle Cotton	Cotton	Sizes 12, 8, 5	he, me, hq, dmq	—
Perle Silk	Silk	1-strand perle	ha, he, me, ma, hq, dmq	—
Machine Embroidery Rayon	Rayon	40/—	me	—
Unique Twist	Cotton/ polyester	12/2	he, me	—
Merino Virgin Wool	Wool	Sizes 15, 8	he	—

This company does not provide needle size recommendations for all thread types.

WONDERFIL®
SPECIALTY THREADS

WonderFil controls the manufacture of its thread from fiber to finished product. Their long-staple Egyptian cotton threads are double-gassed and mercerized.

Accent is a thick rayon thread with sheen.

Dazzle is a 100% rayon thread with a single strand of metallic.

DecoBob is a cottonized polyester that is slightly heavier than InvisaFil.

Designer is an all-purpose polyester thread intended for use in garment construction.

D-Twist is a 2-ply rayon thread made of 2 twisted 40wt. threads.

Efina is made from 100% Giza 88, an extra-long–staple Egyptian cotton.

Eleganza has a lustrous finish and very low lint.

Ellana is a fifty-fifty blend of merino wool and acrylic.

FabuLux is a strong trilobal polyester thread with a brilliant shimmer. Use it on domestic and higher-speed longarm machines.

Fruitti and Spagetti have a lustrous finish and very low lint.

Hologram is a flat, slitted polyester thread with three-dimensional qualities. Use on a vertical spool pin.

InvisaFil is a very fine, strong thread that can be used by hand and machine.

Konfetti and **Tutti** have a lustrous finish and very low lint.

Master Quilter is a fine, lintless polyester with a cotton sheen.

Mirage is a multicolored rayon thread that is randomly space dyed.

Polyfast is a strong trilobal polyester thread with a brilliant shimmer that will withstand mild bleaching.

Razzle is a 100% rayon thread that can be used in a bobbin.

Silco is a lint-free synthetic cotton thread, similar to rayon, that has a sateen sheen.

Sizzle has 1 strand of rayon and 3 strands of metallic. It is textured and sparkly with a coarse surface that "sizzles."

Splendor is a colorfast rayon thread with a silky finish.

Spotlite is a rayon-based metallic thread that is smooth and soft to the touch.

Ultima is a cotton-wrapped polyester thread with the strength of a polyester filament and the finish of spun cotton. It is designed for quilting and general sewing.

Thread name	Fiber	Wt./ply	Use	Needle size
Accent	Rayon	12/2	he, me, dmq, lq	90/14 or 100/16 topstitch; 4.0 longarm
DecoBob	Polyester	80/2	me, mp, dmq, lq	70/10 microtex/sharps, 80/12 microtex/sharps or topstitch, 75/11 or 90/14 quilting or topstitch; 3.5 longarm
Designer	Polyester	40/—	gs, mp	80/12 universal; not for longarm or handwork
D-Twist	Rayon	20/2	me	90/14 or 100/16 topstitch
Eleganza	Cotton	8/2	he	Not for machine use
Efina	Cotton	60/2	ha, hp, mp, ma, dmq	80/12 microtex/sharps
Ellana	Wool/acrylic	12/2	ha, he, ma, dmq	90/14 topstitch
FabuLux	Polyester	40/3	me, dmq, lq	90/14 quilting or topstitch; 3.5 longarm
Fruitti and Spagetti	Cotton	12/3	he, me, hq, dmq, lq	90/14 or 100/16 topstitch; 4.0 longarm
Hologram	Polyester	—	me	80/12 or 90/14 microtex/sharps, 80/12 or 90/14 topstitch
InvisaFil	Polyester	100/2	ha, epp, ma, dmq, lq	60/8, 70/10, or 80/12 microtex/sharps; 75/11 or 90/14 quilting; 3.5 longarm
Konfetti and Tutti	Cotton	50/3	ha, hp, me, mp, ma, dmq, lq	80/12 microtex/sharps or topstitch, 90/14 quilting; 3.5 longarm
Master Quilter	Polyester	40/3	me, dmq, lq	90/14 quilting or topstitch; 3.5 longarm
Mirage	Rayon	30/2	me, ma, lq	90/14 embroidery or topstitch; 3.5 longarm
Polyfast	Polyester	40/—	me, dmq, lq	90/14 quilting or topstitch; 3.5 longarm
Silco	Synthetic cotton	35/3	me, dmq, lq	90/14 topstitch; 3.5 longarm
Sizzle	Rayon/metallic	8/4	he	Not for machine use
Splendor	Rayon	40/2	me, ma, lq	75/11 embroidery, 90/14 topstitch; 3.5 longarm
Spotlite	Rayon/metallic	40/—	me, dmq, lq	90/14 microtex/sharps or topstitch; 3.5 longarm
Dazzle	Rayon	8/—	he	Not for machine use
Razzle	Rayon	8/—	he	Not for machine use. Use in bobbin.
Ultima	Cotton/ polyester	40/2	gs, mp, ps, dmq, lq	90/14 topstitch; 3.5 longarm

YLI THREADS

YLI Threads uses Egyptian-grown extra-long–staple cotton in their cotton threads. Their cotton thread is dyed in North Carolina, Georgia, or Japan and then finished, wound, and packaged in South Carolina.

Candlelight is a heavier metallic yarn that can be used by hand or in the bobbin.

Elite is a spun polyester thread from Japan. This 40wt. thread is equivalent to a 60/3 count/ply thread.

Fine Metallic Thread is made in Japan and designed for high-speed embroidery and machine quilting. Be sure to adjust the tension and use a soft bobbin thread.

Fusions is a heavyweight cotton quilting thread with 1″ variegations.

Hand Quilting Thread is a glazed cotton that has an additional starch glaze added in Massachusetts. It comes wound on a wooden spool.

Longarm Pro is a strong, heavyweight polyester-wrapped poly-core thread designed for longarm quilting. It is dyed and wound in the United States.

Machine Quilting Thread is a cotton thread designed especially for machine quilting. It is processed in the United States.

Pearl Crown Rayon is thick, lustrous, and designed for hand sewing.

Polished Poly and Variations (the variegated line of Polished Poly) are trilobal polyester threads that are strong and lustrous.

Select glazed cotton thread is thinner than YLI's Hand Quilting Thread. The glazing on both makes the threads smoother and more tangle free.

Silk #100 from Japan is a strong, fine thread.

Soft Touch is a fine cotton thread that can be used by hand and machine.

Unlimited Universal Thread is an all-purpose thread, dyed and wound in the United States. It has a polyester-wrapped poly core.

WhisperTouch is a nylon mono-filament thread that is available in sizes .004, .005, and .006.

Wonder Invisible Thread is a strong, fine, clear monofilament meant for machine sewing. It is available in both nylon and polyester. This thread should not melt with a home iron.

Thread name	Fiber	Wt./ply or size	Use	Needle size*
Candlelight (metallic)	—	Thick	he	—
Elite	Polyester	40/— (60/3)	hp, gs, mp, dmq, lq	—
Silk #100	Silk	100/—	ha	—
Fine Metallic Thread	—	Fine	me, dmq, lq	Metafil or metallic
Fusions	Cotton	27/3	dmq, lq	—
Hand Quilting Thread (glazed)	Cotton	40/3	hq	—
Longarm Pro	Polyester	24/— (Tex 40)	dmq, lq	—
Machine Quilting Thread	Cotton	40/3	dmq, lq	—
Pearl Crown Rayon	Rayon	6/—	he	—
Polished Poly and Variations	Polyester	40/— (Tex 27)	me, dmq, lq	—
Select (glazed)	Cotton	40/2	hp, hq	—
Soft Touch	Cotton	60/2	ha, hp, mp, ma, dmq	—
Unlimited Universal Thread	Polyester	28/— (36/2)	gs, mp, dmq, lq	—
WhisperTouch	Nylon	.004, .005, .006 mm	ma, dmq, lq	—
Wonder Invisible Thread	Nylon	.004 mm	ha, ma, dmq	—

* This company does not provide needle-size recommendations for all thread types.

About the Author

BECKY GOLDSMITH began quilting in 1986. She and Linda Jenkins formed Piece O' Cake Designs in 1994. Becky has found that designing and making quilts, and teaching others how to make quilts, is a better career than she could ever have imagined.

Quilters are wonderful people, and Becky loves being a part of the global quilt world. She wants to thank you for including her in your quilting life!

Visit Becky online and follow on social media!

Website: pieceocake.com

Instagram: @beckygoldsmith

Blog: pieceocakeblog.com

Twitter: @beckygoldsmith

Facebook: /becky.goldsmith.poc

YouTube: /BeckyGoldsmith

Pinterest: /pieceocake

Also by Becky Goldsmith:

MOSBY'S
VISUAL GUIDE
TO
MASSAGE
ESSENTIALS

Mosby Editorial Board and
Sandra Fritz, NCTMB

M O S B Y

Publisher: Kenna Wood
Acquisitions Editor: Eric M. Duchinsky
Managing Editor: Christine H. Ambrose
Production Editor: Stacy M. Loonstyn
Production Manager: Chris Baumle
Art Director: Max Brinkmann
Design: Frank Loose Design, Portland, OR
Manufacturing Manager: William A. Winneberger, Jr.
Photography: Camille Gerace, Cam-Works
Line Art: Beverly Ransom

FIRST EDITION

Printed in the United States of America

Composition by: Frank Loose Design, Portland, OR
Printing/Binding by: R.R. Donnelley & Sons

Mosby–Year Book, Inc.
11830 Westline Industrial Drive
St. Louis, Missouri 63146

Library of Congress Cataloging-in-Publication Data
Fritz, Sandy.
        Mosby's visual guide to massage essentials / Sandy Fritz.—1st ed.
                p.   cm.
        Includes bibliographical references and index.
        ISBN 0-8151-3968-3
        1. Massage therapy.   I. Title.
        [DNLM: 1. Massage—methods.   WB 537 F919ma 1996]
RM721.F754 1996
615.8'22—dc21
DNLM/DLC
for Library of Congress   96-29696
                                        CIP

96 97 98 00 9 8 7 6 5 4 3 2 1

MOSBY'S VISUAL GUIDE TO MASSAGE ESSENTIALS

Sandra Fritz, NCTMB
Founder, Owner, Director, and Head Instructor
Health Enrichment Center
School of Therapeutic Massage and Bodywork
Lapeer, Michigan

Wellness and Massage Therapy Consultant
Center for Anxiety, Depression, and Pain Disorders
Port Huron and Metamora, Michigan

Mosby Editorial Board

Mosby and Sandra Fritz would like to thank the following individuals who have influenced the content and clarity of this text to assure the accurate presentation of information:

CONTENTS

CONTENTS

CONTENTS

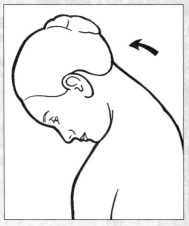

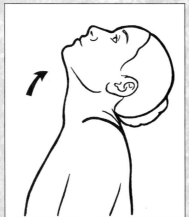

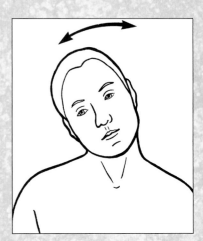

INTRODUCTION

Mosby's *Visual Guide to Massage Essentials* has been developed to educate the consumer about massage therapy, to provide information about the application of non-professional massage shared between family and friends, and to serve as a quick reference guide for the therapeutic massage student or practicing massage professional. This visual guide supports the textbook *Mosby's Fundamentals of Therapeutic Massage*. The reader is encouraged to obtain this text for more detailed and comprehensive information.

This visual guide provides a picture reference of massage methods, organized by application to specific body areas. Content includes suggestions and helpful hints for massage of the head and face, neck, shoulder, arm, hand and wrist, chest, abdomen, back, gluteals and hip, leg, and foot and ankle. Methods for working effectively both on the floor and in a chair are suggested. Information is included about self-massage methods that the consumer can use or the massage professional can distribute to clients for self-help education. Additional information is provided about informed consent procedures, clinical reasoning and problem solving in the therapeutic setting, and common pharmaceutic categories with possible implications for massage.

The basic principles of massage can be learned by anyone interested in self-massage or shared massage in a nonprofessional environment. Professional massage is a therapeutic skill requiring a broad base of knowledge regarding the anatomic and physiologic functions of the human body, the theory and application of massage therapy methods, and the influences of massage on the body processes.

For professional massage practice, knowledge about the interaction of massage with wellness and about the various therapeutic mo-

A group of massage professionals.

dalities and disciplines is essential. To integrate massage successfully with other approaches, an understanding of the theory base of health, training, and service professionals—including medical and osteopathic doctors, chiropractors, physical therapists, nurses, holistic health practitioners, acupuncturists, mental health professionals, athletic trainers, and spa services, among others—is required. The massage professional must also have a basic understanding of nutrition, exercise, stress management (e.g., relaxation methods, communication skills), and pharmacologic intervention. Likewise, the consumer should look for this knowledge base and level of professionalism when selecting a massage therapist.

The massage professional requires, and the consumer should expect, skill in record keeping, charting, informed consent, and assessment procedures. A massage professional must conduct him- or herself ethically; adhere to standards of practice (including business practices); be aware of issues of transference and counter-transference, the boundaries of the professional relationship, and confidentiality. Having an understanding and respect for the scope of practice for massage and other professionals is essential.

Because this text has been written with the massage professional, the massage student, and the massage client or consumer in mind, it reflects a client-centered approach to massage therapy. The client is presented as an educated consumer, able to learn from the therapeutic process and implement the methods into his or her personal life. A reference text of this scope cannot replace a formal educational program using comprehensive textbooks under the direction of a dedicated and experienced instructing staff. This guide can educate the consumer about the professional practice of massage therapy, give the consumer direction in using self-massage and basic massage applications with family and friends, and provide the bodywork student and practicing massage therapist with a valuable quick reference.

For the massage therapist, it is truly amazing how much there is to understand in order to touch in a professional and therapeutic way. There is a necessary balance between head, hand, and heart knowledge that the massage professional must understand. With this knowledge, the professional is better equipped to remain empathetic and compassionate in the therapeutic environment while maintaining appropriate professional boundaries and preventing professional burnout.

Those who share massage in nonprofessional environments can reap many of the same benefits of professional massage. Therapeutic massage is based on the premise of safe, nonjudgmental touch. The values and ethics of professional touch should be respected even in nonprofessional settings.

OVERVIEW

Massage is unique in that it can serve many functions. In its most fundamental form, massage is shared touch between those in intimate and family environments. Basic massage skills can be used to enhance nonverbal communication to convey caring support through a safe and appropriate touch structure. When applied by a trained professional in a deliberate manner, massage is used to accomplish a desired outcome developed between the therapist and the client.

Both professional and nonprofessional massage affects the body in many ways, adding value and comfort to a person's life. Complex physical and emotional situations are best served by trained professionals. Self-massage and nonprofessional massage can be beneficial in managing general daily stress and pain. Many find that professional bodywork is more effective than self-massage for general stress and pain management because it is more comprehensive and focused. The best combination for stress management or management of complex conditions is daily self-massage, shared massage in families and between friends, and regularly scheduled professional bodywork.

Massage can provide a one-hour vacation from daily life by surrounding the body with pleasurable sensory input and shifting the receiver's focus from everyday concerns. Through the professional relationship, massage can provide the benefits of human touch in a therapeutic environment that respects the boundaries of the client. It can

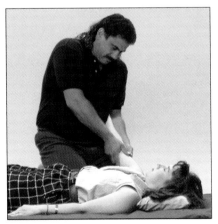

be a key part of a stress management program in a wellness setting or with supervision in a mental health setting for those with anxiety and depressive disorders.

With appropriate training, massage can be a specific rehabilitative therapy used as part of a treatment program supporting the skills of a medical or osteopathic doctor, chiropractor, physical therapist, nurse, or occupational therapist to name a few. Massage can be part of a soothing care program, easing pain and discomfort when supervised as part of the total treatment program. It is beneficial as part of the management of most chronic conditions. Massage can also be a supportive addition to athletic training protocols and exercise programs. Massage can support anyone, from the factory worker to the musician, in the prevention of repetitive strain injury.

Infant massage can be used as a teaching tool to enhance the parental bonding process. Therapeutic touch provides the infant with rhythmic organized sensory stimulation that both soothes the baby and encourages development of the nervous system. Massage can also touch the lonely and isolated individual. Structured touch provides essential human connection and sensory stimulation.

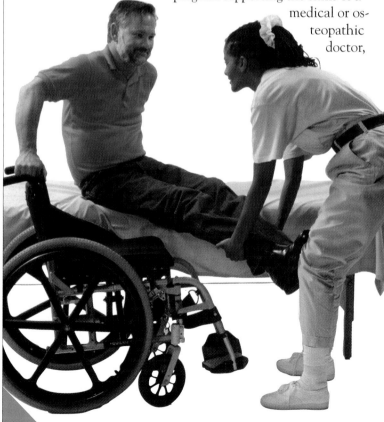

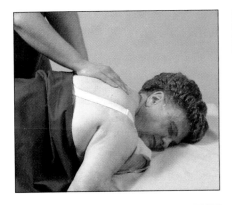

The body responds resourcefully to the simple, repetitive, rhythmic methods of massage. Massage feels good. Research has shown that massage reduces the level of stress hormones, allowing a more balanced physical state that encourages effective sleep patterns and restorative processes. Stimulation of the peripheral and autonomic nervous systems results in subtle yet health-enhancing shifts in the endocrine and neurotransmitter balance that enhances the body's self-healing capabilities.

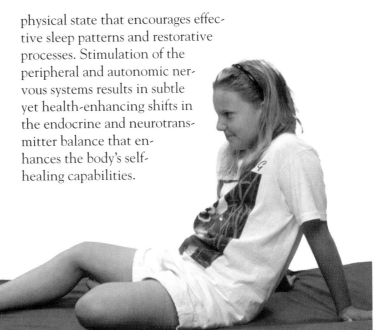

Being in a supportive environment with a caring professional, family member, or friend for an extended period of time may encourage the synchronizing of body rhythms.

Excessive stress or disease causes disorder in the body's natural rhythms (e.g., heart rate, breathing pattern, sleep-wake cycle). When body rhythms become disorganized, order can be reestablished if an organized pattern is followed. The rhythmic and structured application of touch, in addition to being in close physical contact with a calm person with even and ordered body rhythms, provides such an organized pattern. Music and rhythmic movement such as exercise or dance, in addition to a regular daily

The General Benefits of Massage Therapy

Massage manipulation can be applied in a systematic approach or plan to influence conditions that affect physical function.

Skeletal muscles respond with direct biomechanical effects. Within this response, biomechanical effects will encourage or affect reflex reactions that involve the nervous system or chemical responses. The variety of responses is reached at many levels. The nervous system can respond through the reflex arc, the secretion of endorphins and other neural chemicals, and the release of histamine and other cellular secretions. The release of chemical substances affects a structure or system of the body directly or indirectly.

The foundation for the benefits of massage therapy is understanding the nature of the effects on circulation, elim-

ination, and nervous system control. Circulation is improved primarily by direct biomechanical responses to manipulations. A secondary benefit is obtained through reflex responses encouraging chemical secretion or nervous system control.

Circulation improvement delivers nutrients, oxygen, and arterial blood components to the local area being manipulated or to the general circulation. The benefit of circulatory improvement is the secondary effect of improved filtration and elimination of carbon dioxide, metabolites, and biochemical by-products that are transported in the venous blood. Improved circulation, with its ability to affect elimination, generally enhances the abilities of the structures to benefit and support normal function.

Massage manipulations directly benefit restrictions to muscle tissue function. Mechanical benefits and reflex responses combine to help the muscular soft tissues respond through circulation improvement and elimination of by-products. Mechanical effects on the muscular tissues include influence on the stretch receptors, tendon apparatus, and direct manual stretching of the muscle fibers. The reflex effects encourage relaxation of the tissues through change in the motor nerve output and chemical secretions.

Clients receiving massage therapy report a variety of sensations, emotions, feelings, and mental perceptions that are subjective, difficult to measure, and uniquely individual. When nutrition is improved and elimination enhanced, the schedule of exercise, eating, and sleep can also help to order body rhythms and enhance the benefits of massage.

Massage and bodywork application is beneficial in almost all life circumstances. Research shows that it is also health-enhancing to give a massage. Regardless of skill level, massage provides organized, com-passionate, focused touch shared between therapist and client, parent and child, siblings, friends, pets, coworkers, and couples. Massage is always shared touch for the simple reason that you cannot touch without being touched in return.

structures of localized areas, tissues, and systems are given the opportunity to maximize the potential for normal function.

Massage therapy benefits many conditions by encouraging the body through the phases involved in rehabilitation, restoration, and normalization of anatomic and physiologic function and ability. Psychologic benefits occur subjectively and individually in response to therapy, with secondary effects that influence sensation and pain reception. Objective and subjective results of therapy combine to create individual responses that affect the desired health outcome.

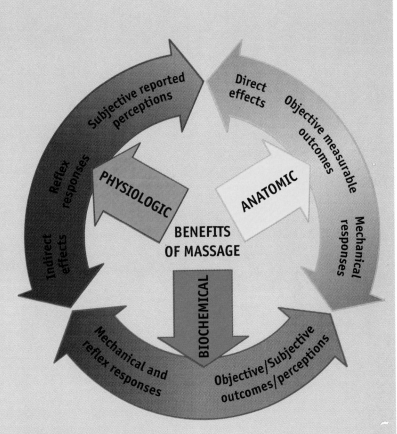

The benefits, effects, responses, and outcomes can occur separately, combined, or as a result of each other.

CONTRAINDICATIONS FOR MASSAGE

The term *contraindication* means either that massage should not be performed or a particular method of massage should not be performed. Regional contraindications are those that are localized. These clients may receive a massage, but a particular area should be avoided. General contraindications mean that massage should not be performed except under strictly supervised conditions under the direction of a health care professional.

Massage consumers must be well informed about their personal

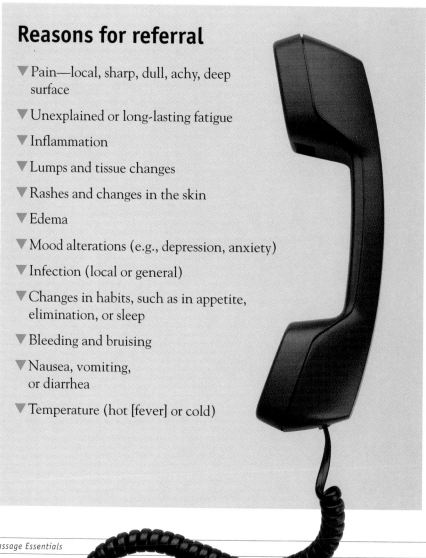

Reasons for referral

▼ Pain—local, sharp, dull, achy, deep surface

▼ Unexplained or long-lasting fatigue

▼ Inflammation

▼ Lumps and tissue changes

▼ Rashes and changes in the skin

▼ Edema

▼ Mood alterations (e.g., depression, anxiety)

▼ Infection (local or general)

▼ Changes in habits, such as in appetite, elimination, or sleep

▼ Bleeding and bruising

▼ Nausea, vomiting, or diarrhea

▼ Temperature (hot [fever] or cold)

health concerns and be able to educate the massage professional about their individual health situation. The information shared with the massage therapist or with any other health care professional is vital to the development of the best possible care plans. It is important for massage consumers to ask questions about the advisability of massage for their personal situation. A professionally trained massage therapist should be educated about contraindications and the need for referral. In general, vigorous massage should be avoided if the recipient is ill for any reason. Gentle massage may be soothing and beneficial. Massage should be avoided over an area of recent injury that is still in an active healing phase. However, massage around this area may promote healing.

Endangerment Sites

Endangerment sites are areas where nerves and blood vessels surface close to the skin and are not well protected by soft tissue. Deep, sustained pressure into these areas could damage the vessels and nerves. The kidneys are included as such a site because they are loosely suspended in fat and connective tissue.

Use light pressure during massage or avoid these areas.

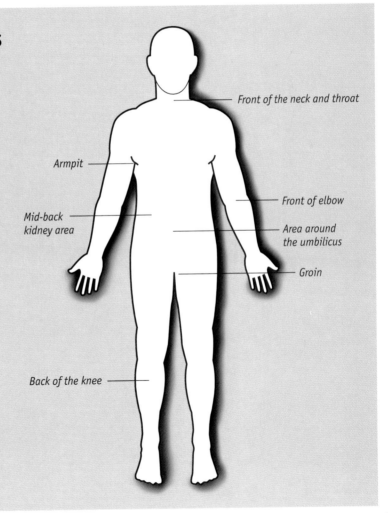

Armpit

Mid-back kidney area

Front of the neck and throat

Front of elbow

Area around the umbilicus

Groin

Back of the knee

ETHICS AND STANDARDS OF PRACTICE

A professional *code of ethics* is a set of moral norms adopted by a professional group to direct choices in a manner consistent with professional responsibility. Professionals have to gauge personal and professional behavior by what is appropriate for the client and the profession as a whole. The massage consumer should expect that the professional who serves them adheres to the following ethical principles:

▼ **Respect**—Esteem and regard for clients

▼ **Client's autonomy or self-determination**—The freedom to decide and the right to sufficient information to make the decision

▼ **Veracity**—The right to the objective truth

▼ **Proportionality**—The benefit must outweigh the burden of treatment

▼ **Nonmaleficence**—Do no harm and prevent harm from happening

▼ **Beneficence**—Contribute to the well-being of the client

▼ **Confidentiality**—Respect for the privacy of information

▼ **Justice**—Equality

Ethical principles direct the development of standards of practice.

Standards of practice provide specific guidelines and rules to form a concrete professional structure. For example, in standards of practice the ethical principle of respect translates into maintaining client privacy and modesty, providing a safe environment, and being on time for appointments. Client autonomy or self-determination becomes informed consent, and ready access to records. Standards of practice guidelines direct quality care, including a structure for measuring the quality of care. Being a professional is a compassionate and caring responsibility. Ethical, professional practice requires a commitment to continued learning, self-reflection, and the highest good for all concerned. It is the right of each client to expect ethical behavior from massage professionals. All professional organizations providing membership for massage and bodywork professionals and the National Certification Board for Massage and Bodywork have professional codes of ethics. Ask to see the code of ethics that the massage professional follows.

Clients are to behave in an ethical manner as well. It is important for respect to be mutual in the therapeutic relationship.

THERAPEUTIC PROFESSIONAL RELATIONSHIP FOR MASSAGE

The therapeutic professional relationship is maintained by the massage professional at all times. A dual or multiple role results from being involved in more than one personal or professional relationship. Dual and multiple roles shift the power base in the therapeutic relationship, making it difficult to maintain professional boundaries. Clients may find themselves becoming dependent on the therapist. This is never appropriate.

Countertransference is the conscious or unconscious emotional response of a therapist to a client that interferes with the therapeutic relationship. Countertransference issues that develop on the part of the massage professional must be dealt with in a way that changes the emotional pattern. If this is not possible the client should be referred to a different therapist. If the client feels that the massage therapist is personalizing the professional relationship in such a way that the client feels uncomfortable, he or she should speak openly with the therapist about the situation. If the situation does not resolve itself the client should seek a different therapist.

Transference occurs when the client personalizes the relationship with the massage therapist. Clients must be aware of their own transference issues and remind themselves of the importance of ethical behavior toward the massage professional. It is unethical for clients to attempt to involve the massage professional in a personal relationship. Professional counseling is sometimes needed to resolve transference feelings effectively.

Maintaining professional boundaries supports compassionate care and continued empowerment of the client. The informed massage consumer understands this professional relationship and supports it.

SCOPE OF PRACTICE

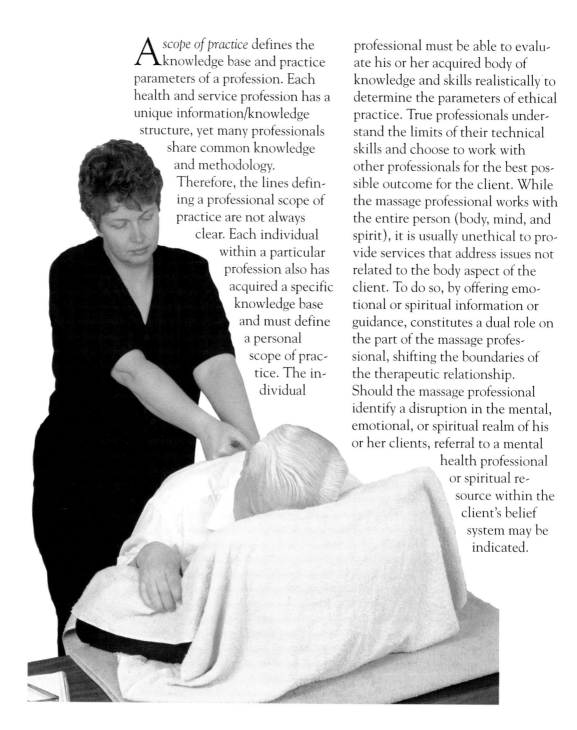

A *scope of practice* defines the knowledge base and practice parameters of a profession. Each health and service profession has a unique information/knowledge structure, yet many professionals share common knowledge and methodology.

Therefore, the lines defining a professional scope of practice are not always clear. Each individual within a particular profession also has acquired a specific knowledge base and must define a personal scope of practice. The individual professional must be able to evaluate his or her acquired body of knowledge and skills realistically to determine the parameters of ethical practice. True professionals understand the limits of their technical skills and choose to work with other professionals for the best possible outcome for the client. While the massage professional works with the entire person (body, mind, and spirit), it is usually unethical to provide services that address issues not related to the body aspect of the client. To do so, by offering emotional or spiritual information or guidance, constitutes a dual role on the part of the massage professional, shifting the boundaries of the therapeutic relationship. Should the massage professional identify a disruption in the mental, emotional, or spiritual realm of his or her clients, referral to a mental health professional or spiritual resource within the client's belief system may be indicated.

Scope of Practice—Therapeutic Massage

	WELLNESS (resourceful functioning with the ability to respond and recover easily)	DYSFUNCTION (functioning with effort with a reduced ability to respond and longer recovery time)	ILLNESS/TRAUMA (functional breakdown with a substantially reduced ability to respond and recover)
BODY Biology—visceral, somatic, anatomy/physiology *Health (body) care professionals* Doctors, physical therapists, acupuncturists, exercise specialists, nutritionists, chiropractors, etc.	Massage therapist has 500+ hours of education Wellness personal service massage without supervision from health care professionals	Massage therapist has 1000+ hours of education Therapeutic massage with consultation or indirect supervision from health care professionals	Massage therapist has 2000+ hours of education Rehabilitation/medical massage with direct supervision by health care professionals as part of a team
MIND Cognitive function—behavior communication, coping skills, stress management, etc. *Mental health professionals* Psychologists, social workers, counselors, etc.	Massage therapist has 500+ hours of education Wellness personal service massage without supervision from mental health professionals	Massage therapist has 1000+ hours of education Therapeutic massage with consultation or indirect supervision from mental health professionals	Massage therapist has 2000+ hours of education Rehabilitation/medical focus with special training in mental health issues; direct supervision by mental health professionals
SPIRIT Purpose, connectedness, hope *Spiritually based professionals*	Wellness personal service massage to bring body/mind connection to spiritual awareness	Supports	Supports

Therapeutic massage is a **body system** that influences mind functions through the body/mind connection and provides an avenue for connecting with a caring professional to support spiritual awareness.

INFORMED CONSENT

Informed consent is a process that protects the consumer and requires that clients have knowledge of what will occur, that participation is voluntary, and that they are competent to give consent. Informed consent is an educational procedure that allows clients to make knowledgeable decisions about whether or not they want to receive a massage, whether they want a particular therapist to work with them, and whether the professional structure, including client rules and regulations, is acceptable to them.

Clients must be able to provide informed consent and demonstrate that they

understand the information presented to them. Parents or guardians must provide informed consent for minors, and guardians must provide informed consent for those unable to do so. According to Corey, Corey, and Callanan in their book, "Issues and Ethics in the Helping Professions," the following questions should be answered at the outset of the professional relationship:

▼ What are the goals of the therapeutic program?

▼ What services will be provided?

▼ What behavior is expected of the client?

▼ What are the risks and benefits of the process?

▼ What are the qualifications of the practitioner?

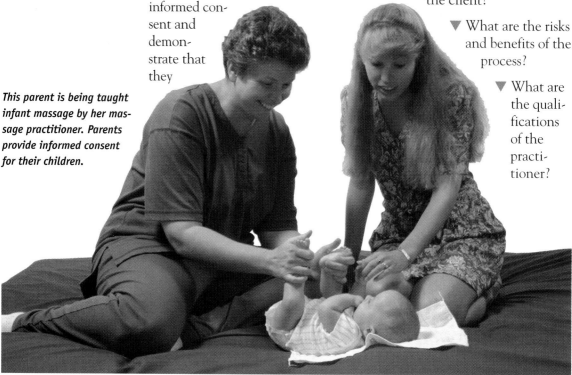

This parent is being taught infant massage by her massage practitioner. Parents provide informed consent for their children.

▼ What are the financial considerations?

▼ How long is the therapy expected to last?

▼ What are the limitations of confidentiality?

▼ In what areas does the professional have mandatory reporting requirements?

True informed consent entails the opportunity to evaluate the options available and the risks involved with each method and requires the massage professional to include information about inherent and potential hazards of the proposed treatment, the alternatives, and the likely results if the situation remains untreated. Clients have the legal right to choose what will be done from a range of suggested options and should have enough information to decide what is the most appropriate approach for them.

Information in client files includes informed consent and charting forms, history and

assessment intake forms, fee and payment records, and, if applicable, the following: signed release of information form(s), authorized communication with client's health care provider(s), and massage therapy treatment orders.

Clients have the right to inspect their files, to have a copy of their files, and to have any information contained in the file explained to them. Massage consumers should expect that client files of this type are maintained. Client files are to be kept confidential but may have to be released under a court order. Bodywork professionals are obligated to report suspicion of abuse and threat of deadly harm to the appropriate authorities.

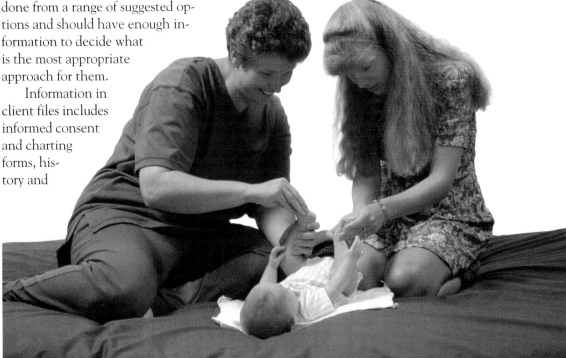

CLINICAL REASONING PROCESS

Therapeutic massage routines do not address the varied needs of individual clients. Instead, each massage session is best designed through a clinical reasoning process. With a combined knowledge of normal functioning, abnormal functioning as determined by the client's history, the client's desired outcome for the massage, and assessment (called *needs assessment*), the massage professional should be able to develop the general massage style and the specific massage approaches that will provide for the best possible restoration and support of normal functioning for his or her client. This information will provide the basis of a care or treatment plan.

Needs Assessment

1. Determine client goals

2. Client history (subjective assessment)

3. Review of referral or authorized reports from the client's health care provider when available

4. Physical assessment, including posture, body symmetry, gait, and palpation (objective assessment)

5. Determination of whether there is a need for a referral (by considering the past history of the client, the client's general health state, and whether there is a logical reason for the client's pattern and symptoms)

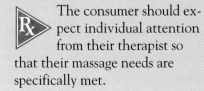 The consumer should expect individual attention from their therapist so that their massage needs are specifically met.

BODY MECHANICS

Giving a massage requires effective use of the body. *Body mechanics* are based on the use of compressive force and body weight (as opposed to muscular strength) to apply pressure. The basic body mechanics principles presented in the illustrations include using a massage table and modified version for massage in a chair and on the floor.

The nonprofessional who regularly shares massage with family and friends may want to consider purchasing a massage table. There are many brands available with costs ranging from $350 to $500 for a standard portable table.

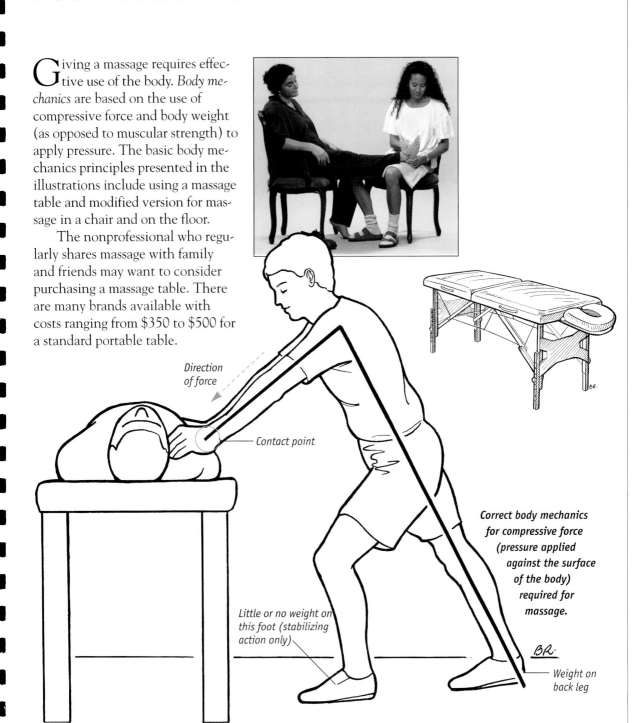

Direction of force

Contact point

Little or no weight on this foot (stabilizing action only)

Correct body mechanics for compressive force (pressure applied against the surface of the body) required for massage.

Weight on back leg

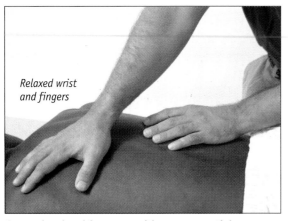

Relaxed wrist and fingers

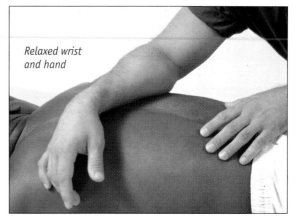

Relaxed wrist and hand

Correct hand and forearm positions are essential.

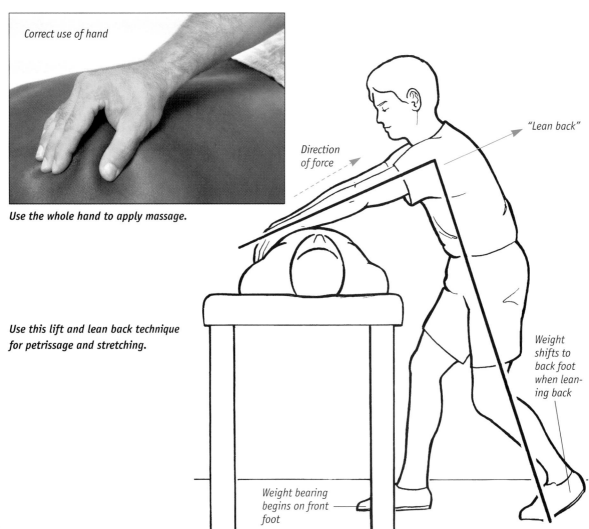

Correct use of hand

Use the whole hand to apply massage.

Use this lift and lean back technique for petrissage and stretching.

Direction of force

"Lean back"

Weight shifts to back foot when leaning back

Weight bearing begins on front foot

MASSAGE LUBRICANTS

There are many massage lubricants available such as oils, creams, and powders. Lubricants are used to reduce friction on the skin during massage. Lubricants should be used sparingly and always dispensed in a contamination-free manner. Unscented products are recommended to avoid allergic reactions.

CLIENT POSITIONING

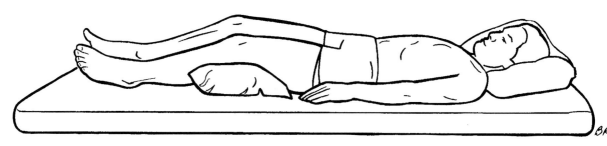

Supine

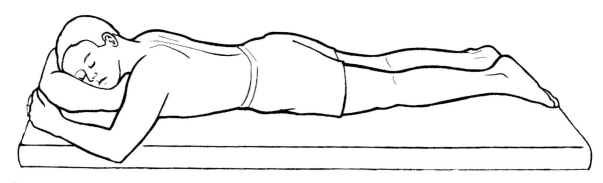

Prone

Side Lying

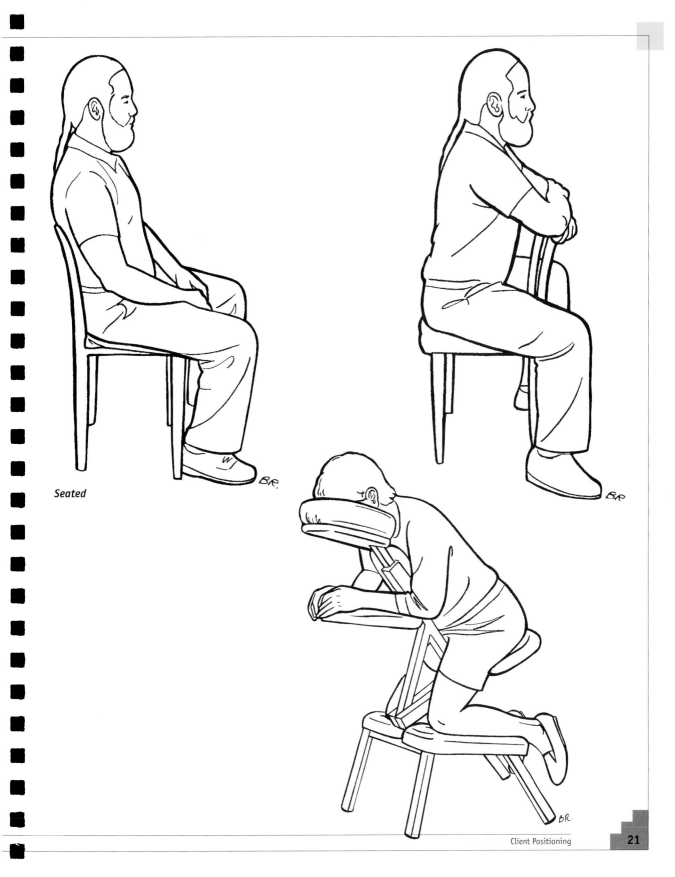

Seated

BASIC DRAPING PROCEDURES

Draping provides warmth for the client, secures the client's modesty, and supports the therapeutic relationship by creating boundaries. Basic draping procedures are illustrated using flat sheets and towels. Only the area to be massaged is undraped. The massage consumer should expect effective and modest draping procedures while receiving a massage.

A.

Client fully draped in prone position.

B.

Drape is folded back to provide access to the back.

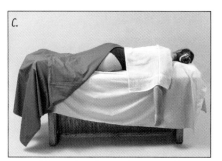

C.

A towel is used to drape the back while the gluteal region is massaged.

D.

Drape is positioned under the leg to be massaged to secure it.

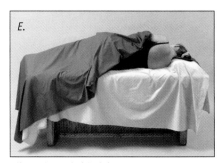

E.

Client draped side-lying.

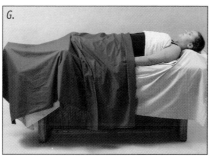

G.

Drape is repositioned over towel.

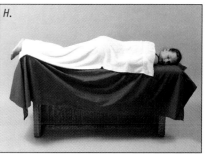

H.

Use of a large towel for draping.

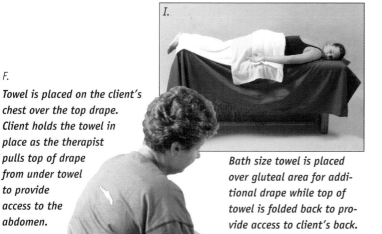

I.

Bath size towel is placed over gluteal area for additional drape while top of towel is folded back to provide access to client's back.

J.

Back is redraped and end corners of towel are folded diagonally to provide access to legs.

F.

Towel is placed on the client's chest over the top drape. Client holds the towel in place as the therapist pulls top of drape from under towel to provide access to the abdomen.

GENERAL CONSIDERATIONS FOR MASSAGE APPLICATIONS

There are many different massage manipulations: effleurage (gliding strokes), petrissage (kneading strokes), compression, vibration, shaking, rocking, tapotement (percussion methods), friction, joint range of motion, lengthening, and stretching. A comprehensive discussion of each method is presented in *Mosby's Fundamentals of Therapeutic Massage*. For the purposes of this book, a simplified approach is used.

Massage strokes glide on the surface of the body, lift or pull soft tissue (muscles and connective tissue), press down to compress soft tissue, strike the soft tissue as in tapping or slapping, and rock or shake the tissue or the body. Variations occur with changes in amount of pressure and duration of stroke. Although massage strokes tend to be directed toward the heart to assist venous and lymphatic flow, this is not always the case. If the goal is stimulation of arterial blood flow, such as with an athlete or someone with cold hands and feet, then compression over the arteries and away from the heart is used.

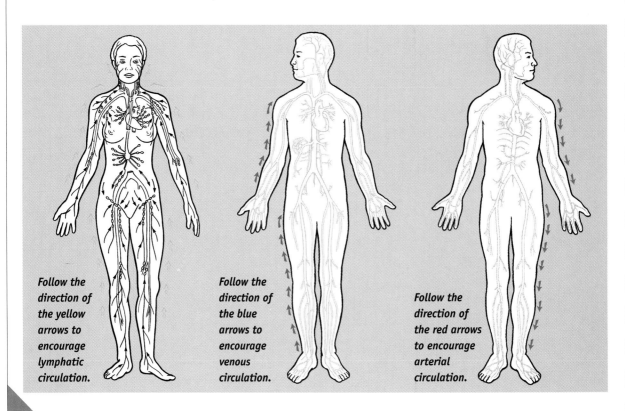

Follow the direction of the yellow arrows to encourage lymphatic circulation.

Follow the direction of the blue arrows to encourage venous circulation.

Follow the direction of the red arrows to encourage arterial circulation.

Range of motion moves the synovial joints of the body. Joint movement can be active, in which the client moves the joint; passive, in which the client relaxes and the massage practitioner moves the joint; or resistive, in which the client moves the joint against a resisting force supplied by the massage practitioner.

Active

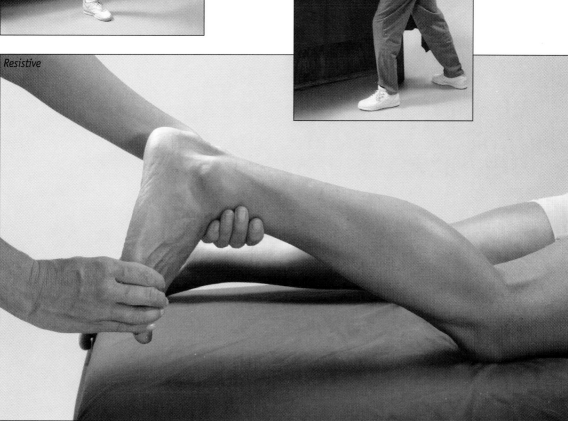

Passive

Resistive

Lengthening methods reestablish the neurologic patterns of the muscles so they can relax. Stretching pulls connective tissue to increase its elasticity and reduce soft tissue shortening. It is important to lengthen muscles first before stretching them or the muscle group may spasm.

Lengthening begins with joint movement patterns. As each joint is moved though its range of motion, some muscles will shorten and some will lengthen. To lengthen a group of muscles purposefully, joint movement patterns should be used to place the muscles in a lengthened position. To affect the nervous system, the client should gently push or pull for a few seconds against a stable resistance provided by the practitioner, then the area should be lengthened gently. There will be an increase in range of motion because the muscle has relaxed. To stretch the connective tissue, begin where the lengthening sequence ended. Before returning the jointed area and the muscles surrounding it to a neutral position, firmly yet gently pull the body area a little farther into the lengthened position. This becomes the point of specific stretching and this position is held for 10 to 30 seconds.

It is also possible to stretch tissue by lifting it away from the underlying bone or structures. This can be done with the muscle and connective tissue at the back of the neck, top of the shoulder, arms, abdomen, hamstrings, and anywhere else the tissue is loose enough to lift. Additional stretching can be added by firmly grasping the tissue with the whole hand and lifting it as far as is possible comfortably. Then, while the tissue is still being held away from the body, move through a gentle range of motion pattern.

Hand contact for lengthening and stretching can become uncomfortable or begin to slip, especially with sustained contact. Using a towel or sheet to grasp the area for lengthening or stretching procedures prevents slipping and provides extra padding for comfort. In general, broad contact with the body, such as with the forearm or the whole hand, feels better than finger or thumb contact (this can feel like being poked). Most people

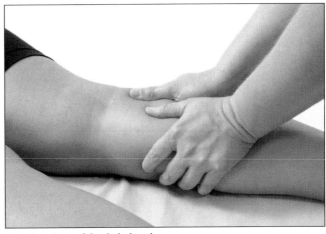
Broad contact with whole hand.

Use of towel to prevent slipping.

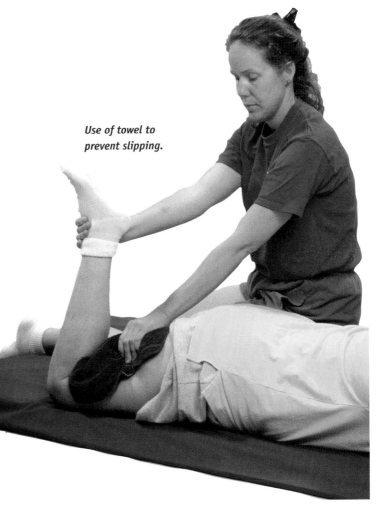

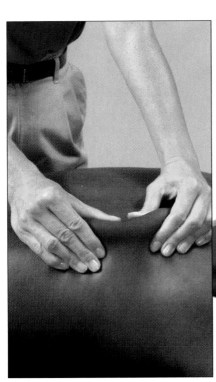
Lifting tissue.

enjoy a firm, even pressure that compresses the tissues. This is best accomplished with the whole hand or the forearm.

Information for the application of massage is organized in the following sections of this book by body area. General relevant anatomic descriptions and suggestions for positioning are provided. Self-massage methods are listed for either the consumer to use or for the massage professional to incorporate into client self-help instruction.

A full body massage will last about one hour. During this time the goal is to massage all of the soft tissues and provide gentle range of motion for the joints. Once the various methods are practiced, a flow pattern can be developed so that the massage has a rhythmic structure.

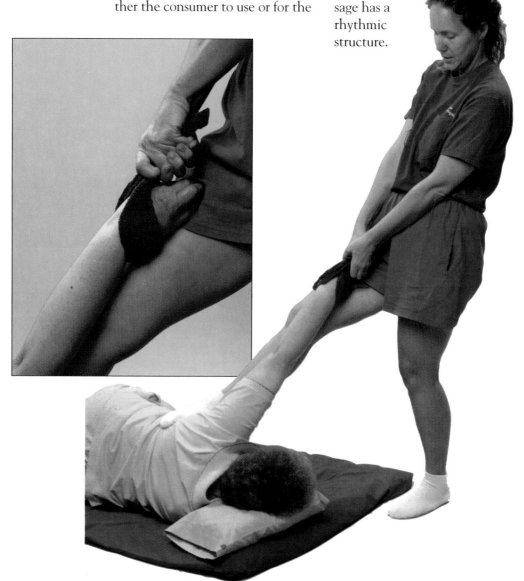

Tender Areas

Tender spots refer to many things, including trigger points, acupuncture points located on meridians (also thought to be neurologic motor points on nerve tracts), and myofacial (connective tissue) microadhesion. Such tender areas are very common and may be encountered while performing massage. Regardless of the type of tender area, pressure against the point for 20 to 30 seconds followed by

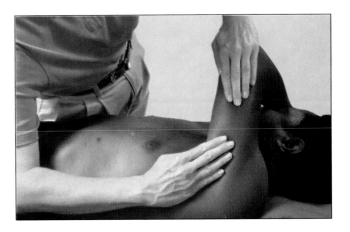

Common Trigger Points

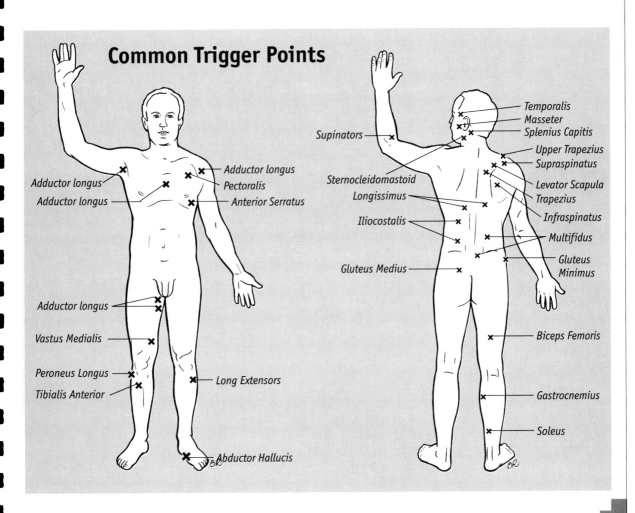

Adductor longus
Adductor longus

Adductor longus
Pectoralis
Anterior Serratus

Adductor longus

Vastus Medialis

Peroneus Longus
Tibialis Anterior

Long Extensors

Abductor Hallucis

Supinators

Sternocleidomastoid
Longissimus

Iliocostalis

Gluteus Medius

Temporalis
Masseter
Splenius Capitis

Upper Trapezius
Supraspinatus

Levator Scapula
Trapezius

Infraspinatus

Multifidus

Gluteus Minimus

Biceps Femoris

Gastrocnemius

Soleus

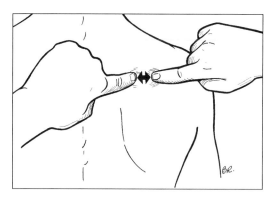

stretching the area is generally helpful. Sometimes simply stretching the skin directly over the tender area is effective. At other times firmly pressing the area together works well. Whenever there is a tender area, it is important to have it evaluated by a professional to rule out a cause other than soft tissue tension.

Stabilization

It is important to stabilize the body while performing lengthening and stretching techniques. The best way to determine the point of stabilization is to move the area into the lengthening or stretching position and notice which other body area moves the most in response to the positioning. The area that moves most indicates the point of stabilization. This point is often over a bony area such as the hip or shoulder. Stabilizing pressure may feel uncomfortable. Discomfort can be avoided by placing a small pillow or folded towel over the area for extra padding.

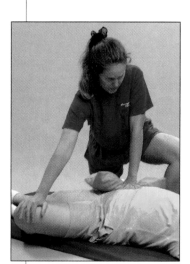

Self-Massage

Massaging oneself can be very effective for stress management and pain control. Because of the way the brain processes sensory input, some forms of self-massage are more effective than others.

In the brain are areas called the somatic sensory cortex and the motor cortex. The *somatic sensory cortex* determines the source and quality of various sensory stimuli. The *motor cortex* activates voluntary muscular movement. The body is represented in both of these areas. Because of the number and sensitivity of nerve receptors, the brain does not see the body as we do. The hands, fingers, face, lips, and feet are the most sensitive body areas, and therefore larger in the brain's view of the body than the legs, arms, back, and chest.

This is important when we consider what areas will respond best to self-massage. Because the hand has such a large sensory and motor distribution, during self-massage the brain neurologically will pay the most attention to the sensations coming from the hand. When an individual massages his or her own neck, which has little sensory distribution, the brain tends to interpret the stronger sensation from the hand. This is why it feels better if someone else massages your neck. When someone gives us a massage, the brain is not splitting sensory signals and can pay full attention to the feeling coming from the area being massaged.

If we massage our own hands, face, and feet, the sensory information from the hands and the area being massaged is more balanced. This allows the brain to pay attention to both the area being massaged and the hand doing the massage work. Using massage tools helps because it eliminates the hand sensations and allows the brain to concentrate on the area that is being massaged.

GENERAL MASSAGE SUGGESTIONS

Body Hair

Excessive body hair requires an alteration in the massage procedure. Gliding and kneading methods can pull the hair, and a lubricant may feel uncomfortable.

The use of compression, vibration, rocking and shaking, coupled with lengthening and stretching procedures, is effective.

Skin Problems

People who may have rashes, acne, psoriasis, or other skin problems also require an alteration of massage procedures. The integrity of healthy skin prevents the transmission of pathogens. However, for people with skin problems physician referral and approval may be required. Massage can usually be provided by placing a clean white bath towel over the affected area and using compression methods over the towel. Be very careful to avoid contact with any body fluids.

Working over a clean towel or sheet can also be helpful for those who have sensitive skin and find the movement of massage irritating. Any method that does not glide on the skin can be used over a towel, sheet, or loose nonrestrictive clothing. Using a towel to lift tissue allows for an effective grip and is more comfortable.

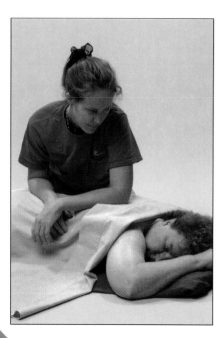
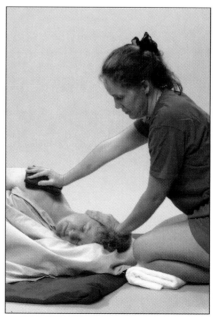

Tickling

Tickling can usually be avoided by reducing the speed and increasing the pressure of the stroke. In addition, because it is difficult to tickle oneself, placing the client's hand on the area to be massaged and massaging with it often solves the problem. Tickling can often be avoided by working over a towel or sheet.

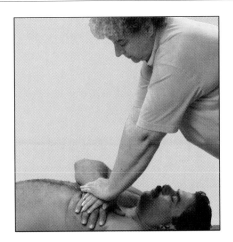

Self-Massage Tools

These everyday household items make excellent and inexpensive massage tools.

▼ Various sizes and densities of balls (i.e., tennis balls, golf balls, soft balls)

▼ Marbles

▼ Tube socks

▼ Wooden knobs

▼ Rubber mats, foam, or towels rolled up to 3- and 6-inch diameters around a 1-inch wooden dowel

▼ Rolling pin

▼ Bicycle tire innertubes

▼ One-, two-, and five-pound rice or sand bags

▼ Frozen vegetables in plastic bags for ice packs

GENERAL MASSAGE SUGGESTIONS

Sanitation

Always wash your hands and forearms thoroughly with hot water and soap before and after giving a massage. Do not massage over breaks in the skin. If the person giving the massage has a break in his or her skin, a latex glove should be worn. Do not come in contact with body fluids. Clean all massage equipment and linens with a 10% bleach solution.

Designing the Massage

The considerations and suggestions for massage presented in the following illustrations and photographs provide a visual smorgasbord of ideas. Sample the different methods and then create your own recipes and application combinations based on these suggestions. Working with these basic methods will help you to generate additional ideas for the application of massage. Being willing to experiment, so long as care is taken never to cause any harm, is essential in the process of learning.

MASSAGE FOR THE HEAD AND FACE

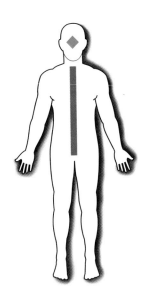

Considerations and Suggestions

▼ Care must be taken before disturbing the recipient's hairstyle and makeup. Always ask before massaging the head and face.

▼ Careful use of lubricants is necessary due to the sensitivity of the facial skin. Lubricant on the face should be avoided if possible.

▼ The delicate nature of the facial skin and muscles requires a confident yet gentle touch.

▼ The extensive motor/sensory sensitivity of the face enables massage to stimulate a large amount of nervous system activity that may be beneficial for relaxation and pain control.

▼ The facial muscles create the expressions that reflect our mood and emotions. Changes in expression are processed in the emotion centers of the brain. Careful attention during massage of the face may gently interact with how the massage recipient feels emotionally.

 The massage therapist must always clean his or her hands before massaging the face. Pathogens can be spread easily through the mucous membranes of the eyes, nose, and mouth. Direct contact with these areas should be avoided.

MASSAGE FOR THE HEAD AND FACE

 **SELF-MASSAGE**

The face is easy to massage yourself. The high neurologic activity of the hands and face make self-massage effective. A one- or two-pound bag of rice wrapped in a towel and placed over the face, just above the nose, provides an effective compression that many find relaxing.

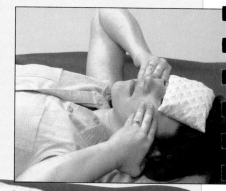

Methods of massage for the head and face

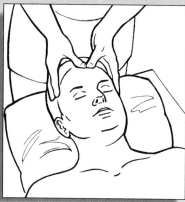

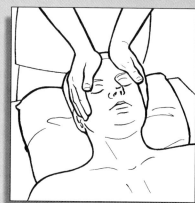

Methods of massage for the head and face

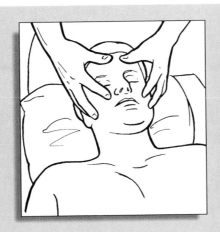 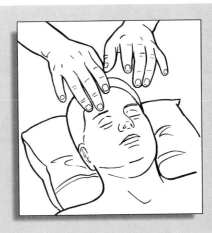

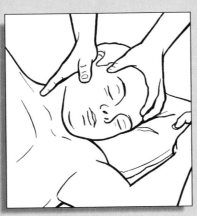 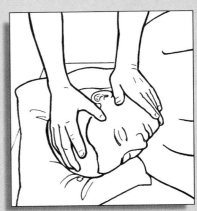

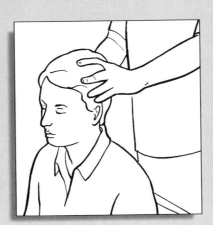 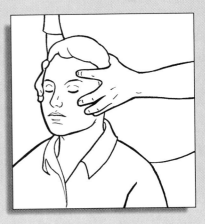

MASSAGE FOR THE NECK

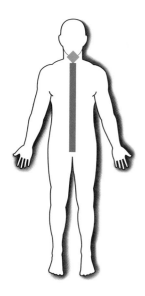

Considerations and Suggestions

▼ Side lying is the most effective position for massage of the neck. In this position the head is stabilized against the table, and the neck area is opened up for easy access.

▼ Lengthening and stretching for the neck from the shoulder should always be provided with the head stabilized. Injury may result if the neck is lengthened or stretched by moving the head.

 Deep pressure into the anterior triangle of the neck (the general area between the sternocleidomastoid muscle and the trachea) should be avoided. Damage to blood vessels and nerves located in this area can result. Broad and gener-

alized methods of massage using the forearm or the whole hand feel less invasive than using fingers and thumbs when massaging the neck.

▼ The neck is a crowded and complex area. It can be affected by responses to stress and by chest and shoulder breathing, which can cause the neck muscles to become rigid and tense. Effective massage of the neck is necessary to provide for relaxed breathing and reduced stress perception.

▼ Careful study of the anatomy of the neck shows that the direct soft tissue influence extends from the forehead, to mid-chest, the back between the shoulder blades, and the middle of the

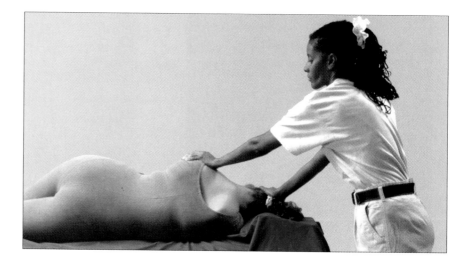

upper arm. Because the neck area balances the head against gravity, postural distortion anywhere in the body will be reflected in the neck. Massage to this area, in conjunction with an entire body approach, is most beneficial.

▼ The brachial nerve plexus begins in the neck. It is helpful to think of most arm, wrist, and hand problems as beginning at the neck. Problems result from either a direct dysfunction of the neck or from difficulties in the arm and hand, which often indirectly cause neck problems.

 ## SELF-MASSAGE

A massage tool for the neck can be made by placing two tennis balls in a long sock and securing them (with knots) in the position that best fits the neck. A section of the sock should be left at each end to use as a handle. You can either lie on the floor with the balls under your neck and use the handle to move the position of the balls or roll back and forth on the tennis balls. In an upright position the balls can be used to massage the neck by placing them against the neck and pulling on the handles. The effect can be increased by rolling the neck back on the balls in a half-moon pattern against the pressure.

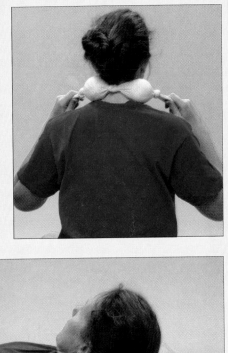

MASSAGE FOR THE NECK

 SELF-MASSAGE

Tilt the head straight back to slacken the tissue at the back of the neck. Using one hand, firmly squeeze the tissue at the back of the neck and lift it as a cat would lift a kitten. Still holding the tissue tightly, roll the neck forward in a half-moon pattern. Attempt to hold the stretch for 30 seconds. Because this is a connective tissue stretch, the feeling may be intense and slightly uncomfortable.

Range of Motion for the Neck

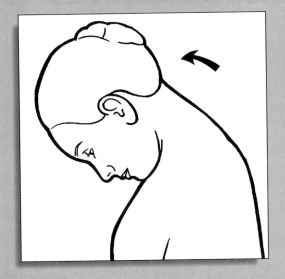

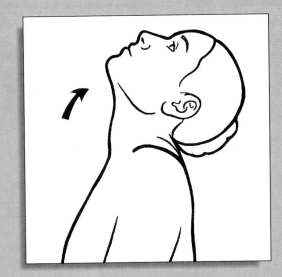

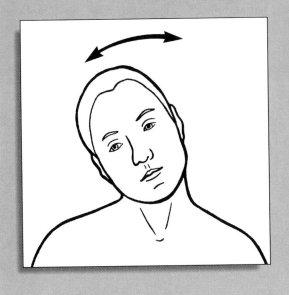

MASSAGE FOR THE NECK

Methods of Massage for the Neck

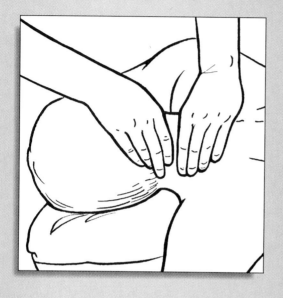

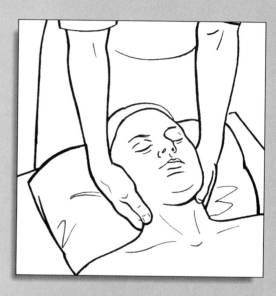

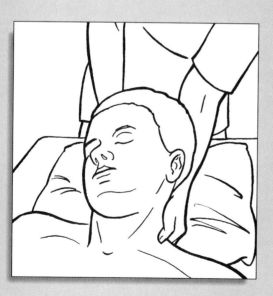

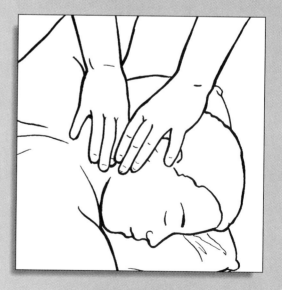

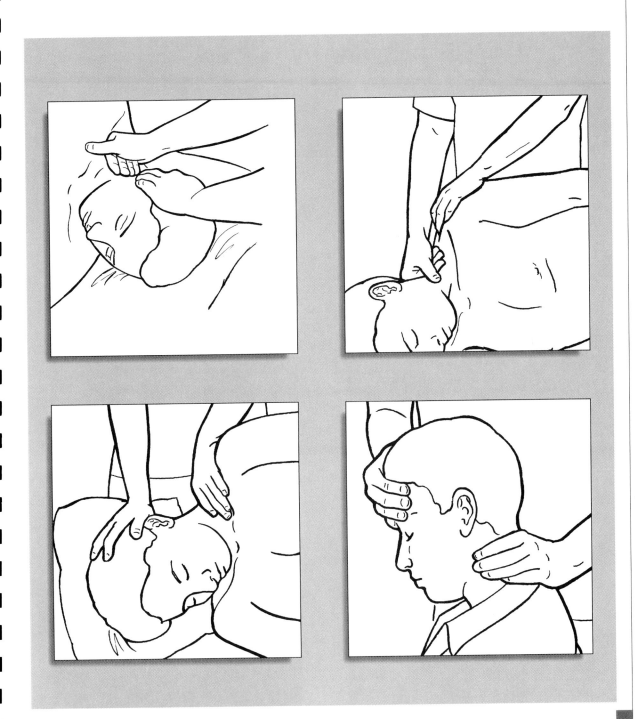

MASSAGE FOR THE SHOULDER

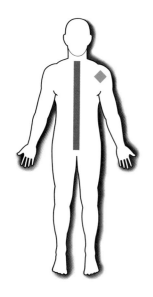

Considerations and Suggestions

▼ The side-lying position is most effective for massage, range of motion, lengthening, and stretching of the shoulder. The shoulder complex (scapula, clavicle, humerus, and associated muscles, ligaments, and tendons) floats on the trunk. It is constructed with a loose fit at the shoulder (glenohumeral) joint to provide for a wide range of motion. Soft tissue (muscles, tendons, ligaments, and fascia) connects the shoulder to the trunk with multidirectional forces coming from the back, chest, and neck. All of these areas need to be considered when providing massage to the shoulder.

▼ The shoulder is stabilized at the iliac crest and sacrum by the latissimus dorsi muscle and the lumbar dorsal fascia. Massage to the low back area should be considered during shoulder massage.

▼ The brachial nerve plexus, which supplies the arm, may be affected by soft tissue dysfunction in the shoulder area. This is a very important consideration for those with arm pain and discomfort, which often results from repetitive use injury. Massaging the shoulder may help reduce muscle tension and soften connective tissue in this area, which could alleviate discomfort in the shoulder and arm.

SELF-MASSAGE

Range of motion is the most effective method for self-massage of this area. Moving against resistance increases the effectiveness of massage. A bicycle tire innertube can be used to provide the resistance, and its circular shape lends itself to many different movement positions.

Because the shoulder is stabilized at the hip and low back area, self- stretching by bringing the elbow above the head and bending to one side is effective. Changing the angle of the elbow and the direction of the bend addresses the multidirectional aspects of the tissue in this area.

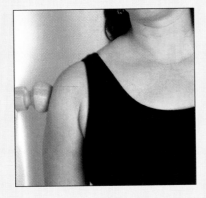

SELF-MASSAGE

A wood knob mounted on the wall at shoulder height can provide a stable force to push against. Using a ball of some type on the floor and lying or rolling on the ball can also be effective.

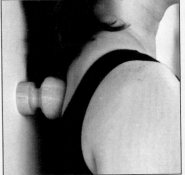

MASSAGE FOR THE SHOULDER

Range of Motion for the Shoulder

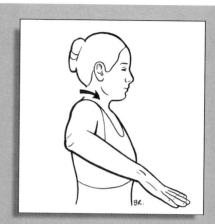

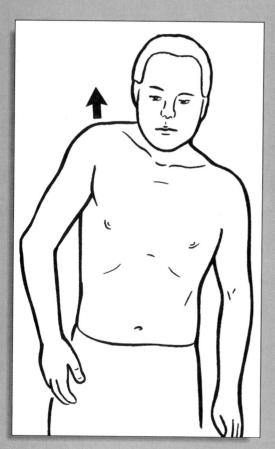

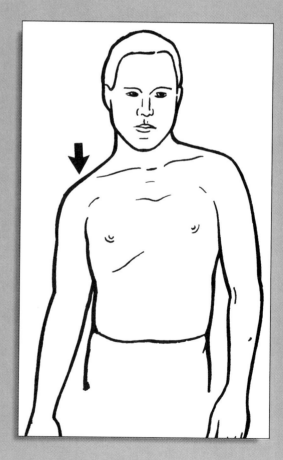

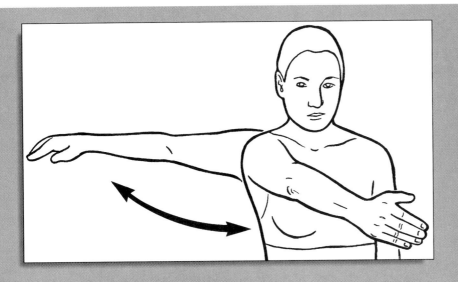

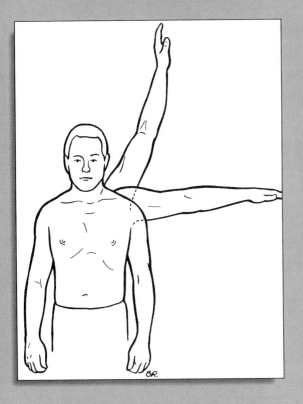

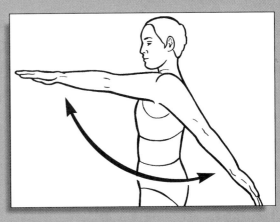

MASSAGE FOR THE SHOULDER

Methods of Massage for the Shoulder

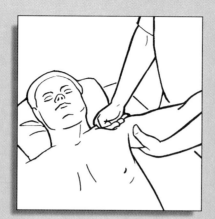
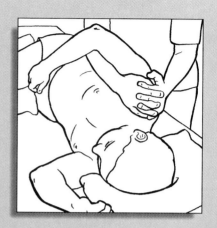
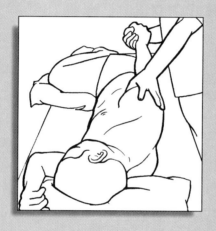
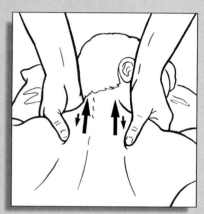
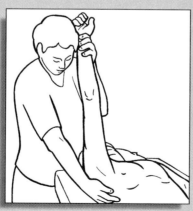
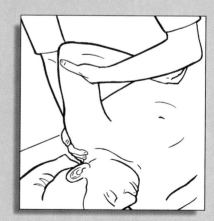

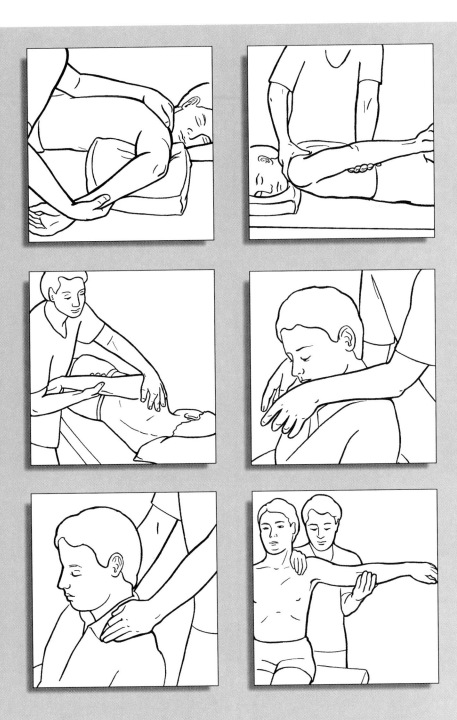

MASSAGE FOR THE ARM

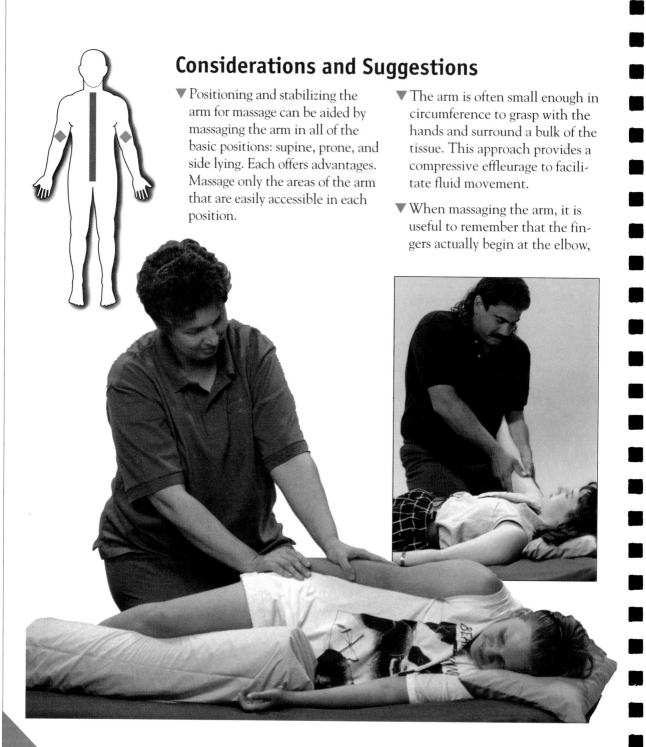

Considerations and Suggestions

▼ Positioning and stabilizing the arm for massage can be aided by massaging the arm in all of the basic positions: supine, prone, and side lying. Each offers advantages. Massage only the areas of the arm that are easily accessible in each position.

▼ The arm is often small enough in circumference to grasp with the hands and surround a bulk of the tissue. This approach provides a compressive effleurage to facilitate fluid movement.

▼ When massaging the arm, it is useful to remember that the fingers actually begin at the elbow, and the shoulder mechanism extends to the elbow.

▼ The elbow joint area is more complex than a hinge joint because of the pronation (palm down)/supination (palm up) action at the elbow. Flexion, extension, pronation, and supination movement patterns must be considered when massaging the arm.

▼ The nerves of the brachial nerve plexus run the entire length of the arm. Nerve impingement from soft tissue at the neck, shoulder, or anywhere on the entire length of the arm should be considered in case of arm pain. Ongoing pain is best addressed by the appropriate medical professional. Basic massage may alleviate some of the symptoms temporarily. A combination of medical care, professional massage, and self-care is the most effective approach.

SELF-MASSAGE

Place the arm to be massaged on a firm surface. Use the opposite hand or forearm to apply compression to the arm being massaged. To massage the tissue, supinate and pronate the arm between the compression and the firm surface. Another method is to firmly grasp the arm to be massaged with the opposite hand and supinate and pronate the massaged arm. Move up the arm with the grasping hand until you reach the elbow.

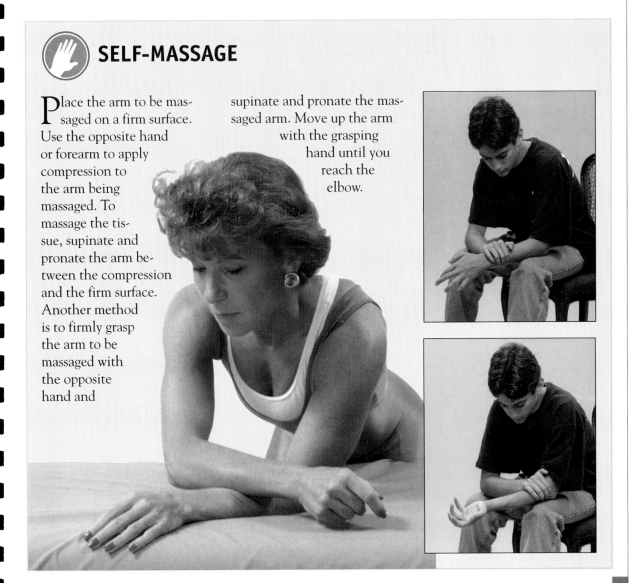

MASSAGE FOR THE ARM

Range of Motion for the Arm

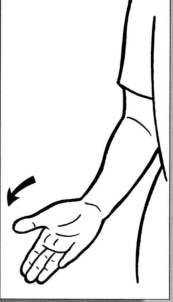

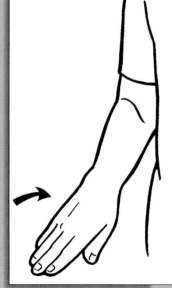

Methods of Massage for the Arm

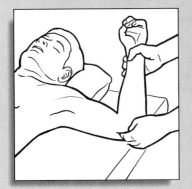
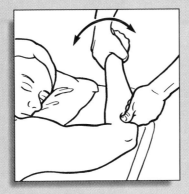
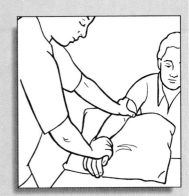

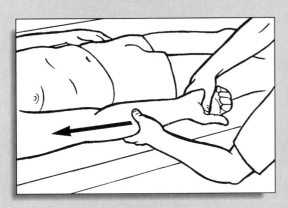

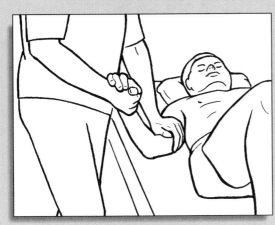

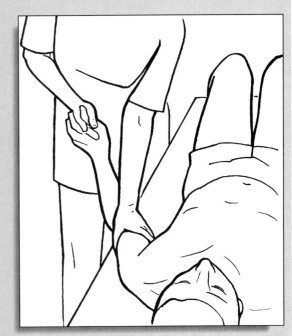

MASSAGE FOR THE HAND AND WRIST

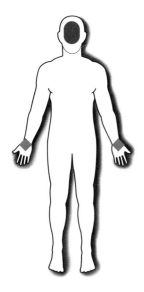

Considerations and Suggestions

▼ Because the hand is usually in a flexed position, opening and spreading the tissue of the palm is very beneficial. The use of compression to provide a pumping action on the palm stimulates the lymphatic plexus in the palm, which in turn encourages lymphatic flow. This can be very helpful for those whose hands swell.

▼ The hand and wrist have an intricate and complex joint and soft tissue structure. Thorough attention to massage of these structures and range of motion of the hand and wrist require time and a focus on detail. Additional study of the anatomy of the hand and wrist would be helpful.

▼ Slow circumduction (moving in a circle) of the wrists, using both passive and active movements against resistance, accesses the joint movement patterns of the wrist. The carpal and metacarpal (palm) joints of the hand can be addressed with a scissoring action. The phalangeal (finger) joints are hinge joints that respond well to active movement against resistance and passive range of motion.

▼ The extensive motor/sensory sensitivity of the hand provides for intense neurologic stimulation through massage methods. Massaging the hand can initiate relaxation and pain control.

 ## SELF-MASSAGE

It is easy to massage your own hands and it is very calming. People tend to wring their hands when anxious, subconsciously attempting to calm themselves. It is important to be deliberate and slow as you perform the wringing action. Squeezing a ball or playing with clay is effective, especially for the flexor muscles. The extensor muscles need stimulation as well. Place a thick rubber band around the fingertips and thumb. Open your hand against the resistance of the rubber band.

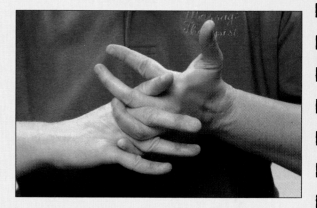

Range of Motion for the Hand and Wrist

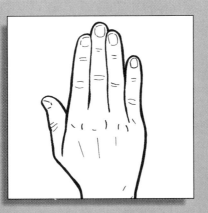
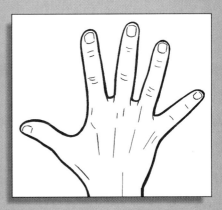
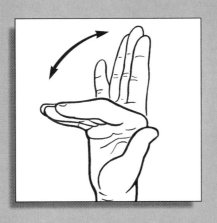
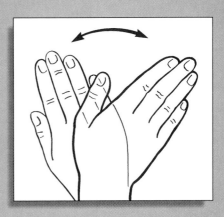

MASSAGE FOR THE HAND AND WRIST

Range of Motion for the Hand and Wrist, continued

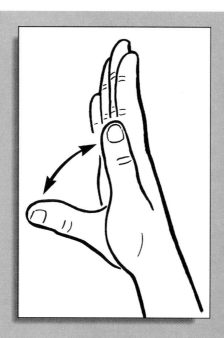

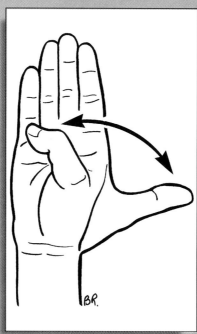

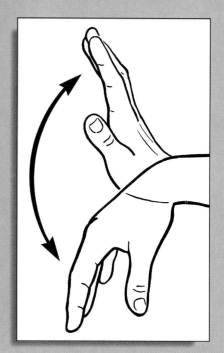

Methods of Massage for the Hand and Wrist

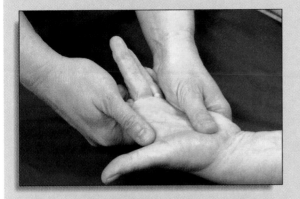

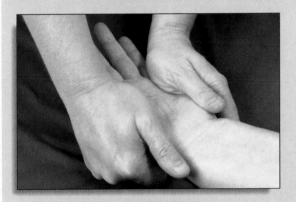

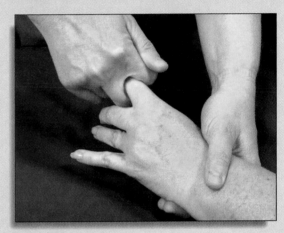

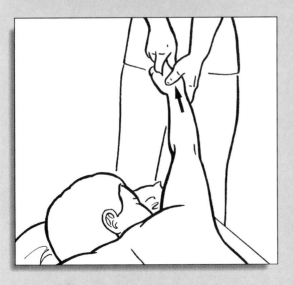

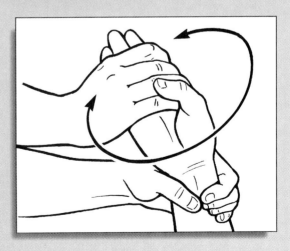

MASSAGE FOR THE CHEST

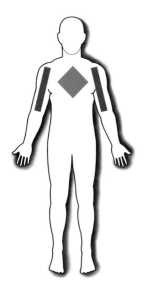

Considerations and Suggestions

▼ The breast area of the female can pose difficulties in accessing the chest area. The side-lying position is effective for massage because the breast tissue falls toward the table, allowing access to the side of the chest and axilla (armpit) area. Using the person's hand to assist you, as you would to avoid tickling, can be helpful when working around the clavicles and ribs. Broad compressive methods to the rib area in the side-lying position are effective in providing general range of motion to the ribs.

▼ Avoid the breast tissue and nipple area on both males and females. During general massage there is no reason to massage this area, and the tissue is often very sensitive to touch and can be irritated easily. Extra attention should be paid to changes in the tissue of the chest area. Without causing any alarm, refer the recipient to his or her doctor if you notice any lumps or tissue changes.

▼ The intercostal muscles (between the ribs) are very important for respiratory function. Slow, deliberate work between the ribs with the client in the side-lying position can be very valuable in restoring mobility and breathing function.

▼ The pectoralis muscles and associated connective tissue are involved in arm and shoulder movement. This large soft tissue area is often shortened, not only affecting arm action but breathing as well. Effective massage, lengthening, and stretching is beneficial.

✋ SELF-MASSAGE

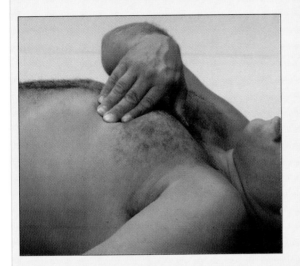

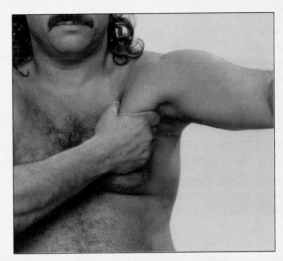

While lying on the back, use the fingertips to massage between the ribs, especially next to the sternum. With one hand, grasp and pull as much tissue in the armpit as possible. Hold the tissue firmly while moving the arm and shoulder slowly through a full range of motion.

Lie prone or on your side with a foam cylinder between your chest and the floor, and roll back and forth on the floor. By changing the angle and position, you can massage the chest. When you find an area that is tender, stop and let the pressure of the weight of your body provide compression and direct pressure. It is beneficial to lengthen and stretch the area after direct pressure.

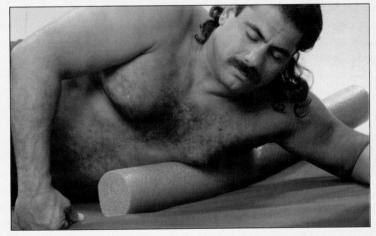

Place weighted sand or rice bags (two to five pounds) on the upper shoulders while seated and breathe slowly for 15 minutes. The weight on the shoulders helps reduce chest and shoulder breathing, which can lead to hyperventilation and the resulting muscle tension.

MASSAGE FOR THE CHEST

Methods of Massage for the Chest

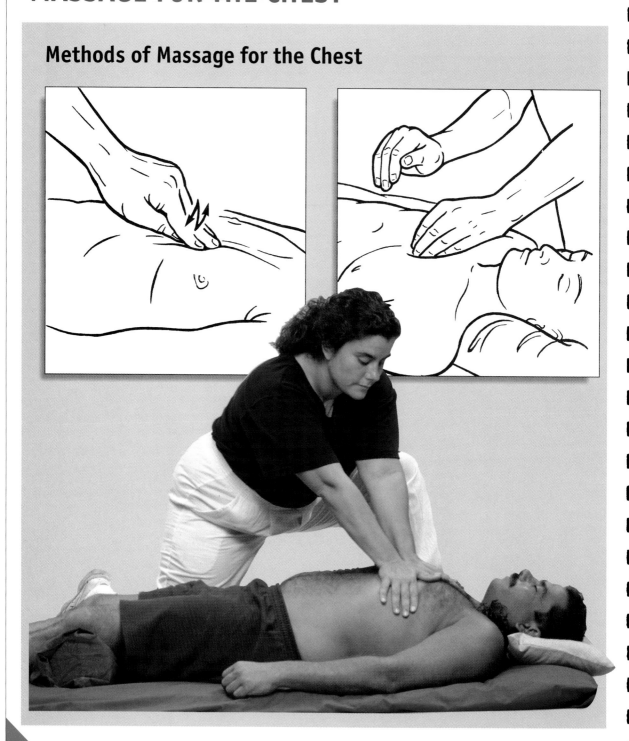

MASSAGE FOR THE ABDOMEN

Considerations and Suggestions

▼ The abdomen can be massaged with the client in the supine or side-lying position. To best facilitate peristaltic movement, follow the pattern in the Methods section. Side lying on the left is the most effective position. During abdominal massage the knees are usually bent about 90 degrees to the trunk to tilt the pelvis and allow the abdominal muscles to relax.

▼ Because there is no bony structure in the abdomen against which to apply pressure, much abdominal work is done with lateral pressure so that the tissue is pushed against pressure from the therapist's opposing hand or with kneading that lifts the tissue.

▼ There is an expansive fascial (a type of connective tissue) system in the abdomen. Lifting methods to stretch this connective tissue can be very beneficial. Using a towel to lift the abdominal tissue provides grip and protects against pinching.

▼ The abdomen is often ticklish. This is a protective mechanism. Follow the instructions for tickles (see page 33). Be careful of putting too much pressure on the abdomen. Always move slowly, allowing the tissue to soften under the touch. If you feel a pulse or throbbing immediately decrease the pressure.

MASSAGE FOR THE ABDOMEN

SELF-MASSAGE

The methods illustrated in the Methods section can be adapted easily for self-massage. Rolling a large, softball on the abdomen is also effective.

Methods of Massage for the Abdomen

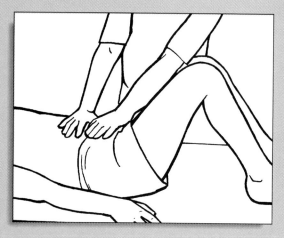

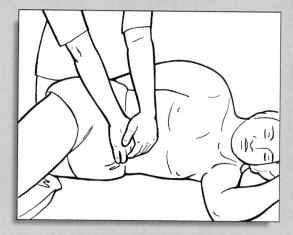

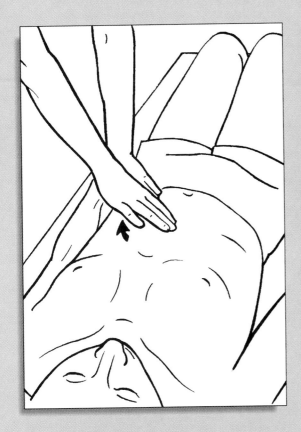

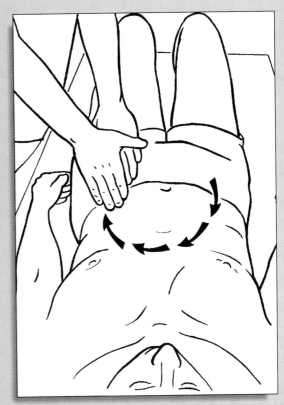

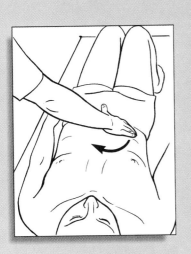

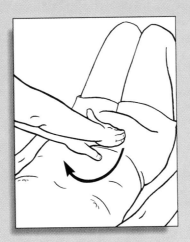

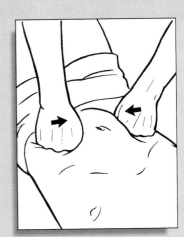

MASSAGE FOR THE BACK

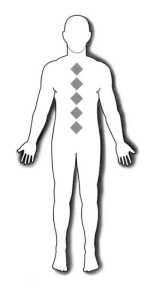

Considerations and Suggestions

▼ The cause of pain or tightness in the back is often shortening and weakness in the chest and abdomen. A change in posture to compensate is often responsible for the back tension.

▼ The back can be massaged effectively with the recipient in the prone, side lying, or seated position. Use of the forearm is very effective for back massage. The lumbar dorsal fascia responds well to skin rolling (tissue lifting) and connective tissue stretching methods. Pressure over the spine is not appropriate. However, skin rolling techniques that lift the skin over the spine are effective.

▼ The low back, including the deep quadratus lumborum muscle, is easily massaged in the side-lying position with the recipient's arm raised over his or her head to lift the rib cage away from the iliac crest. Deep, even pressure with the forearm often feels best to the recipient.

▼ Gentle range of motion to provide for rotation of the spinal column is most effectively done in the side-lying position. Nerve roots are located all along the spine. Massaging close to, but not on, the spine is beneficial.

Range of Motion for the Back

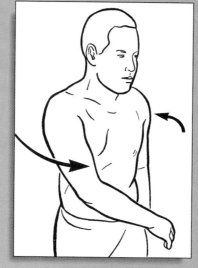

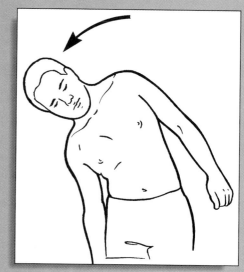

SELF-MASSAGE

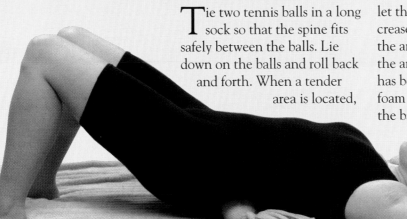

Tie two tennis balls in a long sock so that the spine fits safely between the balls. Lie down on the balls and roll back and forth. When a tender area is located, let the body weight slowly increase direct pressure against the area. Lengthen and stretch the area after direct pressure has been applied. Using a rolled foam or rubber mat to massage the back by rolling on it is especially effective.

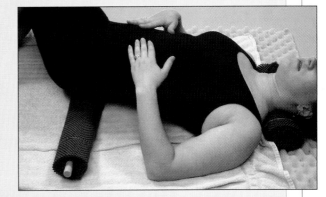

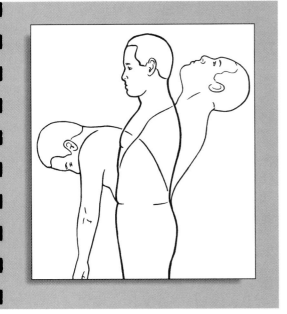

MASSAGE FOR THE BACK

Methods of Massage for the Back

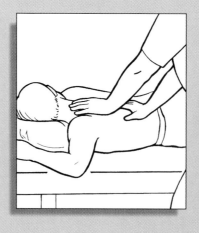
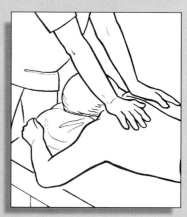
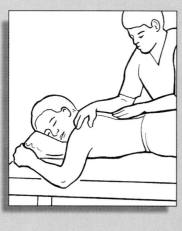
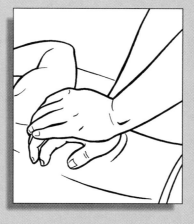
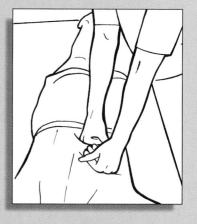
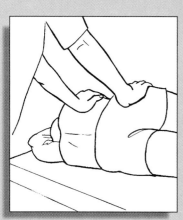
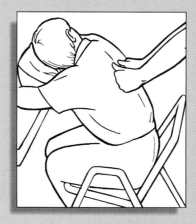

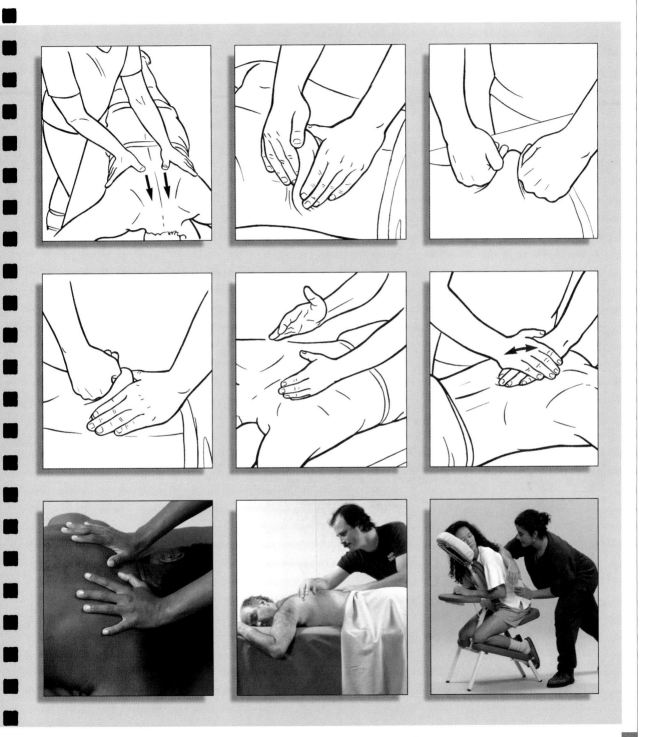

MASSAGE FOR THE GLUTEALS AND HIPS

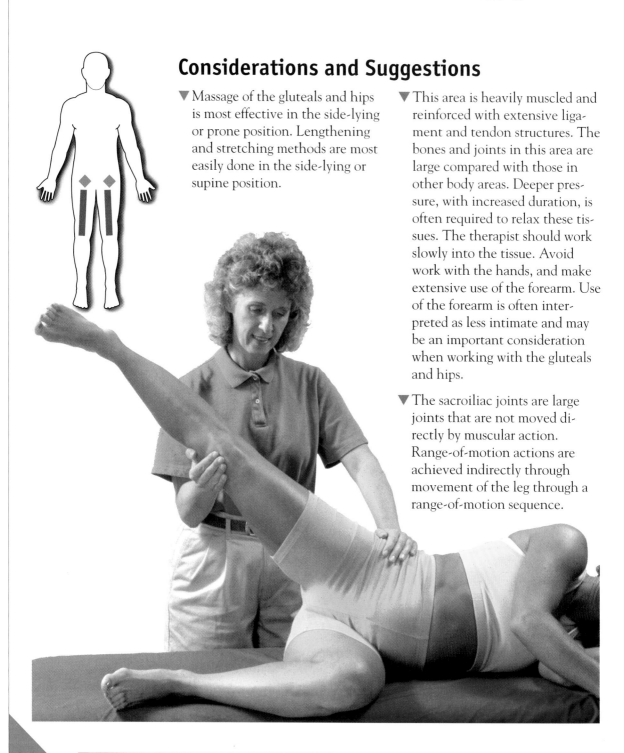

Considerations and Suggestions

▼ Massage of the gluteals and hips is most effective in the side-lying or prone position. Lengthening and stretching methods are most easily done in the side-lying or supine position.

▼ This area is heavily muscled and reinforced with extensive ligament and tendon structures. The bones and joints in this area are large compared with those in other body areas. Deeper pressure, with increased duration, is often required to relax these tissues. The therapist should work slowly into the tissue. Avoid work with the hands, and make extensive use of the forearm. Use of the forearm is often interpreted as less intimate and may be an important consideration when working with the gluteals and hips.

▼ The sacroiliac joints are large joints that are not moved directly by muscular action. Range-of-motion actions are achieved indirectly through movement of the leg through a range-of-motion sequence.

The hip joints are massive joints with extensive ligament structures. The joint provides considerable range of motion second only to the shoulder joint. When using range-of-motion massage methods, include as many variations of flexion, extension, abduction, adduction, and internal and external rotation as needed to involve all of the soft tissue elements.

The lumbar and sacral plexuses supply this region with nerves. Nerve distribution patterns include the entire lower body. The largest nerve is the sciatic. When using heavy pressure to work with the soft tissue, avoid sustained deep pressure on the nerve tracts.

 ## SELF-MASSAGE

Rolling on soft balls works well. When an area of tenderness is located, let the body weight slowly increase the pressure, providing a compressive force against the area. Do not maintain the pressure for longer than 30 seconds at a time to protect any nerves in the area. Reduce the pressure for 60 seconds and then repeat. The area should be lengthened and stretched after compression. Rolling on rolled foam or rubber mats to massage gluteals and hips is also effective.

MASSAGE FOR THE GLUTEALS AND HIPS

Range of Motion for the Gluteals and Hips

Methods of Massage for the Gluteals and Hips

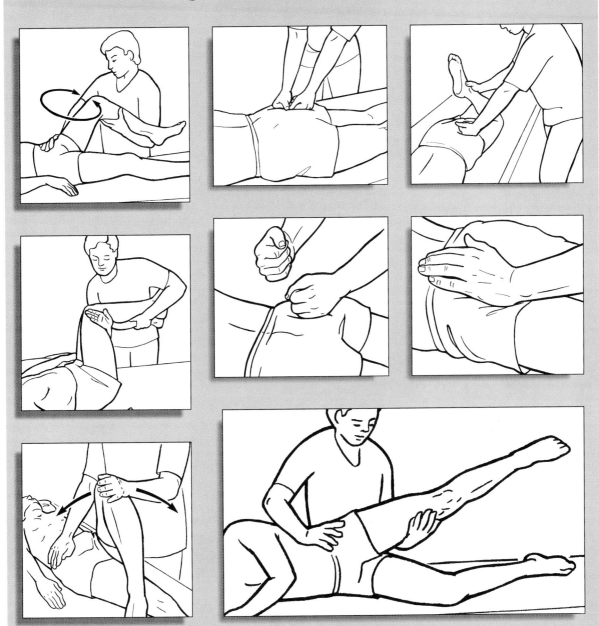

MASSAGE FOR THE LEG

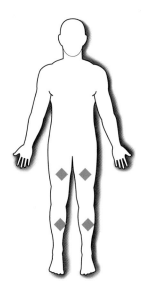

Considerations and Suggestions

▼ Supine, prone, and side-lying are all effective positions for massage of the leg and are best used in combination to easily access all parts of the leg. For the most efficient use of time in the massage session, make sure that each area of the leg is massaged only once. For instance, if massaging the back of the leg in the prone position it is not necessary to massage the back of the leg again in the supine position unless there is a specific reason for doing so. The side-lying position offers the easiest access in the medial and lateral aspects of the leg. The supine position provides access to all aspects of the leg whereas the prone position is the most limited.

▼ The soft tissue mass of the leg lends itself to massage using the forearm. Kneading on the leg is often uncomfortable because of body hair and the tight adherence of the skin and superficial fascia to the underlying tissue. Effleurage and compression are effective methods to use instead.

Varicose veins occur most often in the leg, particularly in the saphenous veins. Thromboembolism and thrombophlebitis are serious conditions involving a blood clot in a vein. If the clot moves it can lodge in the heart, lung, kidney, or brain and cause severe problems. Symptoms of deep vein thrombophlebitis in the legs are aching and cramping that can be mistaken for muscle pain. Massage of any type is contraindicated, and immediate referral is indicated for varicose veins, thromboembolism, and thrombophlebitis. Diagnosis is beyond the scope of practice for massage therapists. Therefore, remain cautious of any leg pain and refer accordingly.

▼ Range of motion for the leg above the knee is the same as hip range of motion. The massage recipient should be effectively stabilized at the pelvis. Stabilizing pressure in this area can be uncomfortable. The use of a small pillow or folded towel over the stabilizing point provides comfort.

▼ The knee is a complex joint influenced by muscles from above and below the joint. Knee instability is often compensated for by increased muscle tension in the leg muscles and thickening and shortening of the iliotibial tract (large connective tissue structure on the outside of the leg). This is resourceful compensation, and the protective nature of the muscle and connective tissue tension needs must be considered. When massaging the leg of someone with a hypermobile knee, the proper methods can reduce excessive muscle tension and connective tissue shortening but should not seek to remove the splinting action entirely. To do so may result in increased knee pain.

▼ The lumbosacral plexus nerves supply the leg, with the sciatic nerve running the entire length of the leg. Impingement can occur anywhere along the nerve pathways. The distribution of leg pain can indicate which nerve portion is affected. When located, the entire

nerve tract must be searched above and below the impingement site for soft tissue restriction to provide soft tissue normalization around the nerves. Light stroking along the nerve tracks is very soothing.

 ## SELF-MASSAGE

In a seated position cross one leg over the other so that the lower leg and ankle are in contact with the thigh. Use the crossed leg to massage the other leg. Drop the crossed leg down so that the calf is in contact with the knee of the opposite leg. Use pressure against the knee to massage the calf. In the seated position the forearm can also be used for self-massage of the leg. A rolling pin works well for self-massage of the legs. It is especially effective for massaging the iliotibial band as well as the lateral side of the thigh.

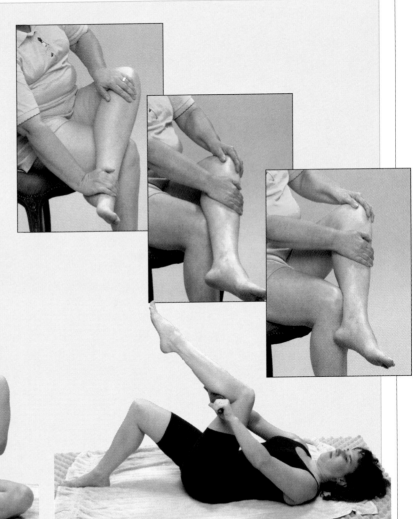

MASSAGE FOR THE LEG

Range of Motion for the Leg

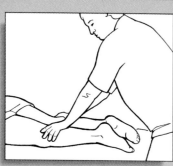

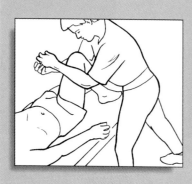

Methods of Massage for the Leg

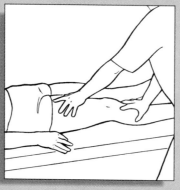

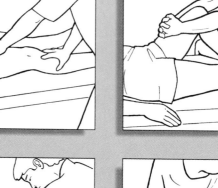

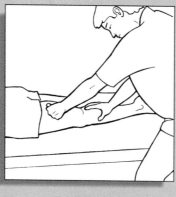

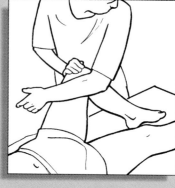

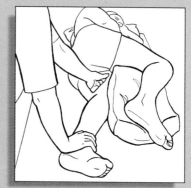

MASSAGE FOR THE FOOT AND ANKLE

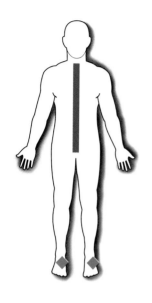

Considerations and Suggestions

▼ The foot and ankle mechanism is a highly complex structure. Its many joints, muscles, and nerves serve to provide stability and the neurologic positional information used during walking and standing. There is an extensive connective tissue network to provide stability. Any disruption of normal foot and ankle action often results in a compensatory pattern through the entire musculoskeletal system. Effective massage attention to the feet is very beneficial. Additional study of gait (walking) patterns and foot anatomy is recommended.

▼ Massage of the foot is one of the best ways to accomplish a high degree of nervous system input to provide for relaxation or pain control. Foot massage has many beneficial effects because it stimulates parasympathetic activity, which results in the relaxation or quieting response. The feet are often a safe area to begin a massage for someone who is nervous or in pain.

▼ Because of the number of joints in the foot and ankle, careful and deliberate range-of-motion work is beneficial in this area.

Slow circumduction, both passive and active against resistance, accesses the ankle movement patterns. The tarsal and metatarsal (main foot) joints can be accessed with a scissoring or bending movement of the foot. Phalangeal (toe) joints are hinge joints and benefit from both active range of motion against resistance and passive range of motion.

▼ The sole of the foot contains a vast lymphatic plexus that acts as a pump to move lymphatic fluid in the foot and legs. Compression used in a rhythmic pumping action is effective in stimulating the lymphatic system. This type of massage can help with swelling of the lower legs and feet.

▼ Sciatic nerve impingement can be felt into the foot. Nerve pain in the foot can indicate impingement anywhere along the nerve track from the lumbosacral plexus to the foot. Nerve pain in the foot must be addressed with massage of the entire leg.

✋ SELF-MASSAGE

Rolling the feet on marbles is an effective massage approach. Standing on marbles placed in a box provides intense stimulation to the bottoms of the feet. Rolling the feet on a large wood dowel or a golf ball is also a good self-massage technique.

Massaging your feet with your hands is an effective combination. The sensory distribution is similar so the body can pay attention to both sensations without the hands overriding the sensory input. Because both the hands and feet are prime sources of sensory information, massaging one's own feet floods the nervous system with impulses and often blocks sensory input from other areas. This stimulation is excellent for temporary pain control and tension. The heel of one foot can also be used to massage the other foot.

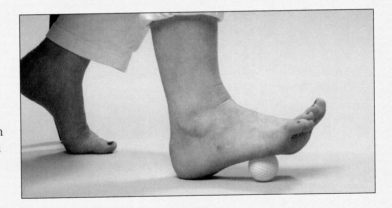

Reflexology is a special area of massage devoted to foot (and hand) massage. This theory relates areas of the foot to body areas as indicated in the following illustration. The benefits of foot massage most likely result from the generalized relaxation response.

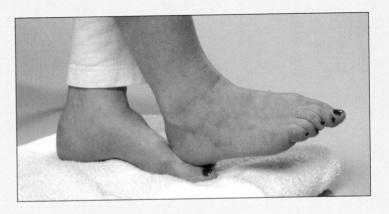

MASSAGE FOR THE FOOT AND ANKLE

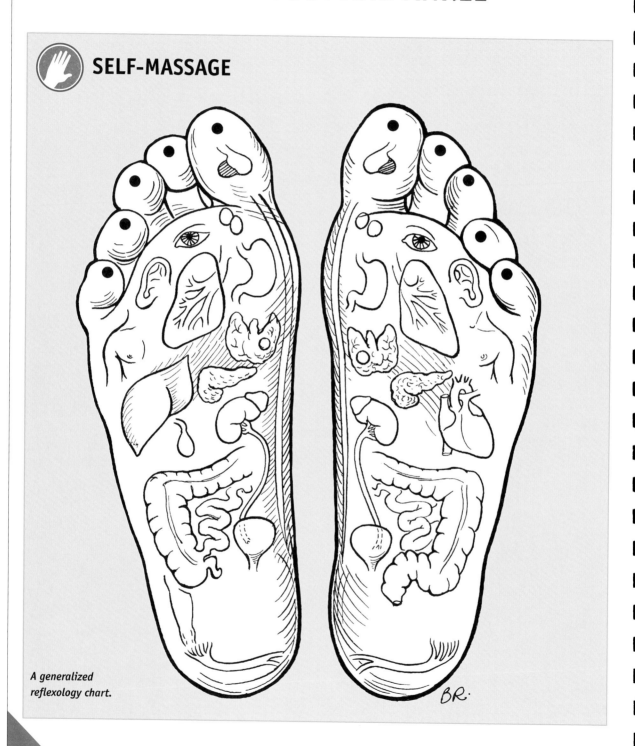

SELF-MASSAGE

A generalized reflexology chart.

BR.

Range of Motion for the Foot and Ankle

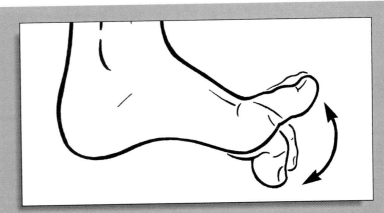

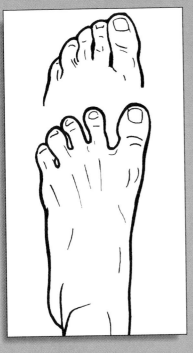

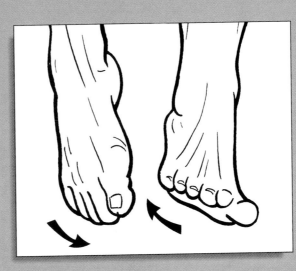

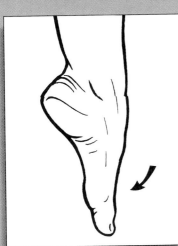

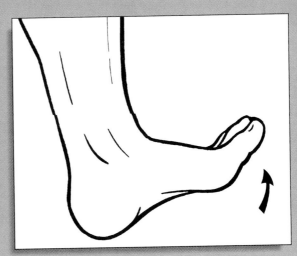

MASSAGE FOR THE FOOT AND ANKLE

Methods of Massage for the Foot and Ankle

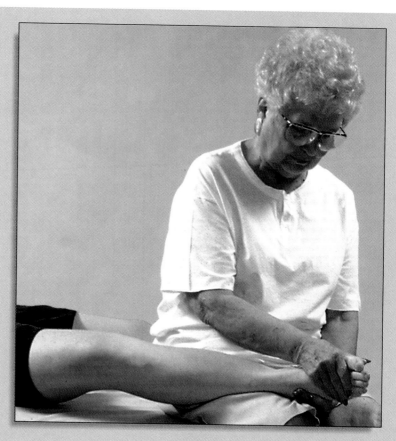

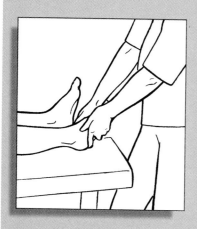

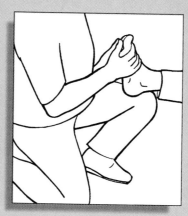

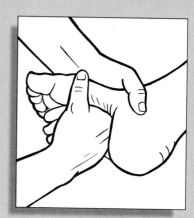

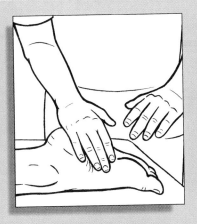

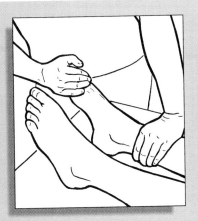

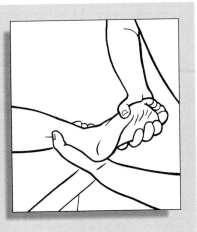

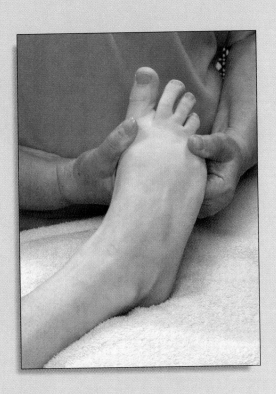

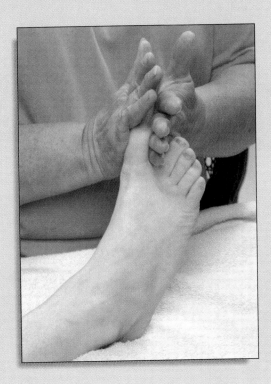

HYDROTHERAPY

Hydrotherapy, or water therapy, is a great addition to massage and can be used easily for self-care. The following information outlines the basics of water applications.

Heat, Cold, and Ice Applications

Effects of heat

▼ Increased circulation

▼ Increased metabolism

▼ Increased inflammation

▼ Decreased pain

▼ Decreased muscle spasm

▼ Decreased tissue stiffness

As a sedative, water is a very efficient, nontoxic, calming substance. It soothes the body and promotes sleep.

Techniques: Use hot and warm baths to quiet and relax the entire body, salt baths, neutral showers to relax body areas, or damp sheet packs.

For elimination, simple immersion in a long hot bath, sauna, or steam room can stimulate the excretion of toxins from the body through the skin. Inducing perspiration is useful in treating acute diseases and many chronic health problems.

Techniques: Use hot baths, epsom salt or table salt for baths, hot packs, dry blanket packs, and hot herbal drinks.

As an antispasmodic, water effectively reduces cramps and muscle spasm.

Techniques: Use hot compresses (depending on the problem), herbal teas, or abdominal compresses.

Effects of cold

▼ Increased stimulation

▼ Increased circulation

▼ Decreased inflammation

▼ Decreased pain

▼ Increased muscle tone

▼ Increased tissue stiffness

Water not only restores the body's normal circulation and temperature, but water treatment, especially with cold water, can also act to restore and increase muscle strength and increase the body's resistance to disease. Cold water boosts vigor, adds energy and tone, and aids in digestion.

Techniques: Use cold water treading (standing or walking in cold water), whirlpool baths, cold sprays, alternate hot and cold contrast baths, showers or compresses, salt rubs, apple cider vinegar baths, and partial packs.

For injuries, the application of an ice pack will control the flow of blood and reduce tissue swelling.

Technique: Use an ice bag, plus compression and elevation.

As an anesthetic, water can dull the sense of pain or sensation.

Technique: Use ice to chill the tissue.

For minor burns, water, particularly cold and ice water, has been rediscovered as a primary healing agent.

Technique: Use ice water immersion or saline water immersion.

To reduce fever, water is nature's best cooling agent. Unlike drugs, which usually only diminish internal heat, water both lowers and removes heat by conduction.

Effects of ice

▼ Decreased circulation

▼ Decreased metabolism

▼ Decreased inflammation

▼ Decreased pain

▼ Decreased muscle spasm

▼ Increased stiffness

Application type

▼ Ice packs

▼ Ice immersion (ice water)

▼ Ice massage

▼ Cold whirlpool

▼ Chemical cold packs

▼ Cold gel packs (caution)

Contraindications

1. Vasospastic disease (spasm of blood vessels)

2. Cold hypersensitivity

▼ Skin—itching, sweating

▼ Respiratory—hoarseness, sneezing, chest pain

▼ Gastrointestinal—abdominal pain, diarrhea, vomiting

▼ Eyes—puffiness of eyelids

▼ General—headache, discomfort, uneasiness

3. Cardiac disorder

4. Compromised local circulation

Precautions

1. Do not use frozen gel packs directly on skin.

2. Do not use ice applications continuously for longer than one hour.

3. Do not use ice applications for treating persons with certain rheumatoid conditions, or for those who are paralyzed or have coronary artery disease.

Ice is a primary therapy for strains, sprains, contusions, hematomas, and fractures. It has a numbing, anesthetic effect and helps control internal hemorrhage by reducing circulation to, and metabolic processes within, the area.

COMMON DRUGS: POSSIBLE INTERACTIONS WITH MASSAGE

The following section will assist in determining what, if any, interaction massage could have with a pharmaceutical. General categories and examples are given in each classification. This is not meant to be an exhaustive list but rather a general guide. Whatever medication, vitamin, or herb a client is taking will need to be researched for the action in the body and possible interaction(s) with massage. This section should provide assistance in that process. Many drugs have similar side effects. Dizziness and constipation are common examples. Massage may help with symptomatic relief for some of these conditions.

Massage consumers should be responsible for monitoring their general condition and informing both the prescribing physician about receiving massage and the massage professional of all medications they are taking. The consumer would benefit by understanding both the intended use and side effects of any medications (including over the counter) they are taking. Someone who is taking many different medications may be best served by working with a massage therapist who has a medical background such as a nurse massage therapist or a massage therapist with advanced training that includes pharmacology. Prescription drugs fall into a number of groups according to the conditions for which they are prescribed.

Pharmaceuticals that may interact with massage

Types of drugs	Effects of drugs	Interaction with massage
CARDIOVASCULAR		
Antianginals	Increase amount of oxygen to heart.	Action of massage has a mild peripheral vasodilation effect.
Vasodilators	Dilate, or widen, blood vessels to enhance blood circulation.	Action of massage has a mild peripheral vasodilation effect.
Beta blockers	Slow heart rate and reduce high blood pressure, or hypertension, by blocking nerve stimulation of the heart.	Effects may be distorted; massage may help with constipation, cause dizziness, or make client susceptible to cold. Client should contract and relax leg muscles before getting off of the massage table.

Types of drugs	Effects of drugs	Interaction with massage
Calcium-channel blockers	Block or slow calcium flow into muscle cells, which results in greater oxygen delivery to the heart.	Expected effects of massage may be distorted or exaggerated; massage may help with constipation or may cause dizziness. Client should contract and relax leg muscles for a minute or two before getting off of the massage table.
Antiarrhythmics	Prescribed when the heart does not beat rhythmically or smoothly.	Joint or muscle pain and swelling may occur; massage may help with constipation and may cause dizziness. Client should contract and relax leg muscles for a minute or two before getting off of the massage table.
Antihypertensives and diuretics	Antihypertensives reduce high blood pressure; diuretics are used in antihypertensive therapy.	Expected effects of massage may be exaggerated and distorted; massage may help with constipation and may cause dizziness. Client should contract and relax leg muscles for a minute or two before getting off of the massage table. The stress-reducing effect of these drugs may affect dosage (contact your physician). Massage increases fluid movement and may enhance the diuretic effect.
Cardiac glycosides	Slow heart rate but increased contraction force; drugs may be used to regulate irregular heart rhythm or to increase the volume of blood pumped by the heart.	Monitor heart rate. Massage slows the heart rate. If rate falls below 50 beats per minute, stop massage and refer client to his or her physician. Regular use of massage may affect the dosage of this drug (seek physician's advice).
Anticoagulants	Prevent blood clotting (blood thinners).	Massage may cause bruising or joint swelling. Massage methods such as compression and skin rolling should be avoided. Massage may interact with dosage of this drug (contact physician).

Types of drugs	Effects of drugs	Interaction with massage
Antihyperlipidemics	Reduce cholesterol levels in order to unclog arteries.	Muscle and joint pain may occur. Massage may help with constipation and may cause dizziness.

GASTROINTESTINAL DRUGS

Types of drugs	Effects of drugs	Interaction with massage
Anticholinergics and narcotics	Block nerve impulses at parasympathetic nerve endings, which prevents muscle contraction and gland secretion; drugs slow action of the bowel and can alleviate diarrhea.	The client's response to massage due to alteration of parasympathetic action may be altered.
Antiulcer medications	Heal ulcers either by reducing production of excess stomach acid or by forming a protective barrier over an exposed ulcer, thus shielding off the stomach acid.	The stress-reduction capacity of massage may enhance the effectiveness of these drugs.

HORMONES

Types of drugs	Effects of drugs	Interaction with massage
Antidiabetic drugs	Induce the pancreas to secrete more insulin by acting on cells that make and store insulin.	Changes in stress levels may affect dosage. Do not provide a vigorous massage because it may cause additional stress on the system.
Sex hormones	Estrogen can be used to treat uterine bleeding and menopausal symptoms; testosterone replaces hormone deficiencies, stimulates red blood cells, and suppresses estrogen reproduction.	Massage can reduce stress levels because emotional states tend to fluctuate with the use of sex hormones. Massage may cause bruising and may temporarily increase fluid movement to reduce fluid retention.
Steroids	May be used to treat inflammatory diseases such as arthritis or to treat poison ivy, hay fever, or insect bites; may be applied directly to skin to treat inflammatory skin conditions.	Changes in stress levels may affect dosage (contact physician). Avoid massage methods that may create inflammation such as friction and skin rolling.
Thyroid drugs	Regulates thyroid activity and metabolic rates.	Changes in stress levels may affect the dose. Clients and physicians should monitor dosage if massage is used on a regular basis.

Types of drugs	Effects of drugs	Interaction with massage
ANTIINFECTIVES Antibiotics	Treat a wide variety of bacterial infections.	Clients should not be exposed to infectious diseases such as the common cold (carefully follow sanitation suggestions and Universal Precautions); avoid overstressing the system when providing massage. Gastrointestinal side effects are common. Massage may calm symptoms temporarily.
Antivirals	Combat viral infections.	Massage has similar effects on all antiinfective drugs (see Antibiotics).
Antifungals	Treat fungal infections to prevent fungal growth.	Massage has similar effects on all antiinfective drugs (see Antibiotics).
Anthelmintics	Treat worm infestations.	Massage has similar effects on all antiinfective drugs (see Antibiotics).
Scabicides	Treat scabies.	Massage has similar effects on all antiinfective drugs (see Antibiotics).
Pediculicides	Treat lice.	Massage has similar effects on all antiinfective drugs (see Antibiotics).
ANTINEOPLASTICS Antineoplastics	Used in the treatment of cancer; prevent the rapid multiplication of cancer cells.	Massage should be administered gently and under the direct supervision of the client's physician.
CENTRAL NERVOUS SYSTEM Sedatives	Reduce the amount of certain chemicals in the brain, thus limiting anxiety and panic disorder.	Massage can increase or decrease the effect of these medications depending on the nature of the massage. Carefully monitor the client during the massage and work in conjunction with the prescribing physician.
Antipsychotics	Treat patients with mental disorders; allow transmission of certain nerve impulses but restrict others.	Massage has similar effects on users of antipsychotics and sedatives (see Sedatives).

Types of drugs	Effects of drugs	Interaction with massage
Antidepressants	Combat depression and migraine headaches; work by increasing the concentration of certain chemicals necessary for nerve transmission in brain.	Massage causes a shift in neurotransmitters and other brain chemicals. Massage will initially have a stimulating effect on the central nervous system. Massage increases serotonin and helps with constipation; work with prescribing physician.

CENTRAL NERVOUS SYSTEM

Types of drugs	Effects of drugs	Interaction with massage
Amphetamines	Reduce appetite, keep person awake, increase heart rate, and raise blood pressure; also used to treat narcolepsy.	Massage has a stimulating effect on the central nervous system even when used for relaxation. Work with prescribing physician to determine changes in dosage; massage can help with constipation.
Anticonvulsants	Control seizures and other symptoms of epilepsy by selectively reducing brain stimulation.	Massage stimulates central nervous system and neural transmitter activity; the relaxation effect is a secondary result of nervous system stimulation. Work with the client's physician to adjust dose when massage is used in therapy.
Antiparkinsonism agents	Correct the chemical imbalance in the brain caused by Parkinson's disease.	Massage has similar effects on users of antiparkinsonism agents and anticonvulsants (see Anticonvulsants).
Analgesics	Treat pain and may cause drowsiness.	Nonnarcotic analgesics such as aspirin thin the blood, and bruising may occur. Pain perception is not accurate when taking analgesics, so feedback mechanisms are unreliable; reduce massage intensity. Massage can help with constipation and cause dizziness; monitor patient carefully.

Types of drugs	Effects of drugs	Interaction with massage
Anti-inflammatory drugs	Relieve muscle pain, inflammation, and spasm; skeletal muscle relaxants are often given in combination with an antiinflammatory drug such as aspirin.	Avoid techniques that create inflammation or damage tissue. Pain perception may be altered, so feedback mechanism are not accurate. Reduce intensity of the massage.
RESPIRATORY DRUGS Antitussives	Control coughs.	Question the client about any over-the-counter medications; avoid heat hydrotherapy. Drugs can cause dizziness, and results may be distorted. Client may be unable to relax after massage.
Expectorants	Change a nonproductive cough to a productive one by bringing up phlegm.	Massage has similar effects on users of all respiratory drugs (see Antitussives).
Decongestants	Constrict blood vessels in the nose and sinuses to open up air passages; raise blood pressure but do not interfere with cilia movement or mucus production.	Massage has similar effects on users of all respiratory drugs (see Antitussives).
Bronchodilators	Open airways in the lungs to allow for easier breathing; can either be inhaled or orally employed.	Massage has similar effects on users of all respiratory drugs (see Antitussives).
Antihistamines	Counteract symptoms of allergy, such as itching and swelling; also used to treat motion sickness.	Massage has similar effects on users of all respiratory drugs (see Antitussives).
VITAMINS AND MINERALS	Chemical substances that are vital to the maintenance of normal body function.	High intake of vitamin supplements may have implications for massage, but individual research would need to be conducted to determine suspected interaction; it is too comprehensive of an information base to detail in this format.
HERBS	Medical plants that act similarly to pharmaceutical drugs.	Question clients about the use of herbs on a case-by-case basis to determine the expected reaction with massage; this is too comprehensive of an information base to detail in this format.

RESOURCE LIST

There is much more to learn about massage and bodywork. It is important to investigate the credentials of a massage professional carefully. The following information will provide some guidance.

Magazines and Journals

Massage Magazine
1315 W. Mallon
Spokane, WA 99201
800-533-4263

Massage Therapy Journal
820 Davis Street
Suite 100 Subscriptions
Evanston, IL 60201-4444
708-864-0123

Books and Videos

Mosby's Fundamentals of Therapeutic Massage
Mosby's Fundamentals of Therapeutic Massage Student Workbook
Mosby's Therapeutic Massage Video Series

In selecting a qualified massage therapist, both the education and professional affiliation of the therapist should be researched. He or she should be a graduate of a state-licensed school that requires at least 500 contact hours. The therapist should also have a membership in a professional organization that requires standards of educational and ethical practice for membership. The three most established organizations are:

American Massage Therapy Association (AMTA)
820 Davis Street
Suite 100
Evanston, Ill 60201-4444
708-864-0123

Associated Bodywork and Massage Professionals (ABMP)
218677 Buffalo Park Rd.
Evergreen, CO 80439-7347
800-458-ABMP

International Myomassethics Federation
17172 Bolsa Chica #60
Huntington Beach, CA 92649
800-433-4IMF

National certification can be checked by contacting:

National Certification Board for Therapeutic Massage and Bodywork
8201 Greensboro Dr.
Suite 300
McLean, VA 22102
800-296-0664

State licensing, if available, can be checked by contacting the department of licensing and regulation in each state.

CONCLUSION

This book has provided a beginning look at therapeutic massage as it is shared between both professionals and nonprofessionals. Also discussed is the training level required to present oneself as a professional massage therapist/bodywork practitioner.

The integrity of touch therapy is maintained in the professional relationship that develops between the massage therapist and the client, each being responsible for maintaining the appropriate boundaries. An informed, responsible consumer and a well-trained practitioner build the best professional partnership.

As with any new skill, it will take time to become competent with the methods illustrated in this book. Continue to practice the techniques and remember that it is difficult to give a bad massage because safe, compassionate touch almost always feels good and is beneficial. Massage provides organized, nurturing, focused touch shared between therapists and clients, parents and children, siblings, friends, pets, coworkers, and couples. As someone once said, "When half the world is giving a massage and the other half is receiving a massage, then maybe we will have peace."

Sandra Fritz

REFERENCES

Consumers Guide Editors: *Prescription Drugs*, Lincolnwood, IL, 1995, Publications International, Ltd.

Corey G, Corey M, Callanan P: *Issues and Ethics in the Helping Professions*, ed 4, Belmont, CA, 1993, Brooks/Cole.

Fritz S: *Mosby's Fundamentals of Therapeutic Massage*. St. Louis, 1995, Mosby Lifeline.

Griffith H: *Complete Guide to Prescription and Non-prescription Drugs*, 1990, Los Angeles, The Body Press Division of Price Stern Sloan Inc.

Keen J, et al.: *Mosby's Critical Care and Emergency Drug Reference*, St. Louis, 1994, Mosby.

INDEX

A

Abdomen, massage methods, 61-63
Abuse, 15
Acne, 32
Acupuncture points, 29
Amphetamines, 88
Analgesics, 88
Ankle: *see* Foot/ankle
Anthelmintics, 87
Antianginals, 84
Antiarrhythmics, 85
Antibiotics, 87
Anticholinergics, 86
Anticoagulants, 85
Anticonvulsants, 88
Antidepressants, 88
Antidiabetic drugs, 86
Antifungals, 87
Antihistamines, 89
Antihyperlipidemics, 86
Antihypertensives, 85
Anti-inflammatory drugs, 89
Antineoplastics, 87
Antiparkinsonism agents, 88
Antipsychotics, 87
Antitussives, 89
Antivirals, 87
Anxiety, 8
Appetite changes, 8
Apple cider vinegar baths, 83
Arm
  massage methods, 50-53
  range of motion, 52
Arterial circulation, 24
Assessment, 16
Athletic training protocols, 4
Autonomic nervous system, 5

B

Back
  massage methods, 64-67
  range of motion, 64
Beneficence, 10
Beta blockers, 84
Biochemical by-products, 6
Biomechanical effects, 6
Bleeding, 8
Body fluids, 32
Body hair, massage and, 32
Body mechanics, 17
Body rhythms, 6
  dance and, 6
  exercise and, 6
  music and, 6
Body self-healing capacities, 5
Body symmetry, 16
Body system, therapeutic massage
    as, 13
Bodywork application, 7
Breathing function, 58
Breathing pattenrs, 6
Bronchodilators, 89
Bruising, 8

C

Calcium-channel blockers, 85
Carbon dioxide, 6
Cardiac glycosides, 85
Care plan, 9, 16
Charting, 2, 15
Chemical responses, 6
Chest, massage methods, 58-60
Chiropractors, 2
Circulation, massage effects on, 6
Clients
  autonomy and, 10
  behavior of, 14